HOW TO START A BUSINESS WITHOUT A COLLEGE DEGREE

ROGER K. DANETH

INTRODUCTION

How often have you thought about starting a business but you think you don't have enough money, or it is too complicated, or you don't have time, or you could not do it by yourself...? There are always excuses for not doing something that takes a little time and effort. A lot of businesses have started in a garage, on the street, or even in a dorm room. You have probably heard of Bill Gates, Michael Dell, Steve Jobs, and Warren Buffet. All of these people started small but put in the time and effort to be successful. Well of course we can't all be geniuses like those people are, and most of us will not achieve their level of success. But always think positive and plan ahead. You never know what you can achieve if you try.

This book will not focus on building a massive business empire, but on small businesses that can be started by an individual, starting with a small amount of money, very limited capital, or even on borrowed money. You don't need to be a college graduate to do any of theses businesses, but you may have to take some short courses to cover certain types of work.

We will suggest a number of simple, but not necessarily easy, businesses that you might be interested in. Keep in mind that no business is easy, and there are always pitfalls to watch out for. Even when you are in business, you still have to earn your living, just like you do if you have a job working for someone else.

Most of the nitty gritty details of starting a business are covered in the Appendix so we don't have to keep repeating it. You can read the Appendix when you are ready. With this understanding we will now start with the meat of this book. To get the most out of this book, you should all the way through it because there are good ideas in each business that you may be able to use in your business.

TABLE OF CONTENTS

4. Backyard Mechanic
5. Buy and Fix Cars for Re-sale
6. Buy a car in the South, Sell in the North
7. Start a Sell-Your-Own Car Lot
8. Home/Office Cleaning and Janitorial
9. Carpet Cleaning and Reconditioning
10. Water Pressure Cleaning
11. Pool Cleaning Service
12. Mold Removal
13. Pest Removal (Varmints)
14. Pest Removal, Insects
15. Computer Systems Network Set-up and Repair
16. Business/Technical Consulting
17. General Contracting, Home Repairs, Remodeling
18. Illustrator
19. Deliver Newspapers
20. Airport Shuttle Service
21. Same Day Local Package Delivery Service
22. Moving and Storage
23. Resume Writing
24. 'Find a Job' Counseling, Using Social Networks
25. Mentoring/Tutoring
26. Business Guidance/Consulting
27. Start an On-Line Store
28. Start a Catalog Business
29. Start a Pyramid Sales Business
30. Freelance Computer Programmer
31. Contract Engineer/Technician
32. Make Custom Hand-Crafted Furniture

33. Restore Antiques
34. Start a Coffee Shop
35. Art Business/Studio
36. Make Gizmos
37. Become a Notary Public
38. Become a Translator
39. Become a Ghost Writer
40. Become a Tutor
41. Become a Contract English Teacher
42. Beauty Counselor (for the ladies)
43. Musician, Performing Arts
44. Yard Decorations
45. Make Boutique Soap
46. Make Specialty Candles
47. Make Jewelry
48. Sell Hot Dogs
49. Start a Pawn Shop
50. Start a Rental Store
51. Become a Head Hunter
52. Catering
53. Food Truck
54. Barbecue Cart
55. Start a Lingerie Online Store
56. Start a Vegetable Stand
57. House Painting
58. Small Repairs on Houses
59.0 Wood Floor Restoration
60. Install Solar Auxiliary Power Systems
61.0 Build Patio Decks
62. Become a Real Estate Agent
63. Become a Real Estate Appraiser
64. Home Assistance

65. Home Insulation Testing and Remediation
66. Home Inspection
67. Provide Services for the Elderly Citizens
68. Home Sitting
69. Interior Decorating
70. Christmas Decorating
71. Publish Books Online
72. Heating, Ventilation, and Air Conditioning
73. Repair Lawn Mowers
74. Life Insurance Agent
75. Make Money out of Junk
76. Lawn Cut and Trim
77. Lawn Weed and Feed
78. Be a Gardner
79. Online Media Store
80. Be a Picker
81. Writing Apps for the iPhone or Android Cell Phones
82. Pet Grooming
83. Photograph Weddings
84. Freelance Photography
85. Pan for Gold
86. Search for Meteorites
87. Start a Guard Business
88. Become a Real Estate Agent
89. Become a Physical Trainer
90. Trade Goods
91. Be a Wilderness Guide
92. Become a Travel Guide
93. Become an Investment Advisor
94. Start a Pizza Business
95. Coil Winding

96. Drive an Ice Cream Truck
97. Make Skin Cream
98. Document Shredding
99. Build a Shooting Range
100. Bow and Arrow Range
101. Sell, Service, and Repair Bicycles

BUSINESS DESCRIPTIONS

1. Audio/Video Installation

This business can be started with a small with a panel truck, a few simple tools, and a knowledge of setting up audio and video equipment. Normally you would do this as a service in someone's home. By the way some stores charge as much as $200 to do this service for a customer. They usually take no more than one hour to do the job. So if you only charged $100 and completed the work in one hour, you would be making $100 per job and beating out the competition.

You may already know how to do this work if you have done it for yourself at your home. Even if you have not done much of it, setting up consumer entertainment equipment is quite simple if you just read the manuals that come with the equipment that the customer has already bought.

There are a lot of people who can't connect a simple cable from one piece of equipment to another, or it just boggles their minds and they want someone to do it for them. Of course the customer buys all the equipment including cables. All you have to do is show up with a small hand tool box and help the customer set it up. The customer is not likely to have certain cables such as TV HDMI cables, and audio signal connection cables. So you might want to carry a stock of these cables in your truck to avoid wasting time having to run to a store to get them.

It can get more complicated if the customer wants to mount his big screen TV on the wall or build components into a wall or a custom cabinet of some kind, but if he does you can quote a high price and then locate a carpenter to help you on contract. As time progresses and you gain experience, you may expand to having an audio/video store where you sell and service certain kinds of high end equipment. But don't try to compete with the same brands that Wal-Mart or other volumes stores sell.

Get listed at the Better Business Bureau and in the Yellow Pages. Get the name of your company, your logo, name and phone number on your panel truck. Your panel truck does not have to be new and shiny. An old truck is fine if it is clean. You might need to give it a paint job to brighten it up. Then the business sign on your truck will look great.

2. Automobile Wash and Detail

I like this business because almost anyone can do it. You don't have to have a building, or commercial lot, to do this kind of work. You only need a full size pick-up truck. You can then go to the customer's home or place of business and do it while the customer is working or not in immediate need of the vehicle. There is one catch. You will need water to wash the vehicle. If you wash a car at a customer's home, you can usually get permission to use his outdoor water faucet. You probably will not have access to water at a place of business. A solution to this problem is to get a truck that has a water tank in the back. Or have a water tank installed in the back of your truck to use. The tank should be strong enough so that you can pressurize it with an air compressor. Be careful, compressed air in a tank is dangerous if the pressure is too high. Even 15 pounds of pressure inside a tank is dangerous if the tank cannot handle it safely. To use an air pressurized tank, you will need a professionally made tank that is designed to handle a certain amount of pressure. A simple alternative is to use a mechanical method of pressurizing the tank such as a hand pump. There are no doubt other ways to make it work. Be innovative. You will need the usual business requirements that I detail in the Appendix.

3. Automobile Battery Service

This is another simple business. Again you don't need a 'brick and mortar' store for the business. You can go mobile, bringing your help and service to the customer's location, whether he or she is stalled somewhere on the highway, or at his home.

All you need is a truck or a van for carrying simple hand tools, a battery tester (Auto-Zone carries them), a jump-start battery box (you can buy one at Wal-Mart), jump start cables, some distilled water for dry batteries, and a few new batteries of typical sizes that you can bring with you and sell to the customer, if he or she needs one. A few spare alternators and drive belts would also be good to have with you. Of course, you charge the customer for any parts or materials you install, and for your labor according to how much time is required, plus expenses like gasoline to and from the job. Make arrangements with a towing service that can help you to have the customer's vehicle towed to a garage, if that is necessary. You can charge the customer for the tow, and then pay the towing company. A lot of times, all that is needed is to clean battery cable clamps and battery terminals, and tighten the clamps on the terminals. A related service you can also provide is repair of flats.

You will need to carry an air compressor and some tire repair tools in your truck for this work. Always give your best service and don't over charge so you will have a good reputation and be recommended to others. Again, be sure to set up your business according to the regular requirements as listed in the Appendix.

4. Backyard Mechanic

If you have knowledge of the mechanics of automobiles, you may be interested in this kind of a business. Usually it is operated informally. Advertising is word-of-mouth to friends, and friends of friends. If you are good, people will say, 'I know someone who can fix your car. Why don't you call his number?' or the equivalent of that. Have business cards printed that you can pass out to your friends.

You have to be careful in this business that you do not tackle a job that is beyond your capabilities. For example, it might take too long for you to fix the problem, or the work requires heavy expensive tools that you do not have available and you don't plan to spend the money for them. Normally, you would look over the potential customer's vehicle, ascertain what is wrong with it, and determine whether or not you really want to work on it. Maybe the engine is very dirty and would just not be fun to work on. If that's the case, 'just say no'. Don't make your work unpleasant for yourself.

You decide where you want to work on the vehicle, and how much you charge per hour. You will charge the customer for your time and any materials or special tools you have to purchase for the job. Do not let a customer have his car back unless he or she pays you fully in cash only. Before you start working on a job, you should make the customer signs a contract, which has your terms and conditions preprinted on it. No checks or credit cards. Make sure the customer understands ahead of time that you will require full payment in cash at the end of the job. It's a good idea to require a cash down payment if the job is extensive, and expensive materials are required. The down payment should at least cover the cost of materials. If the customer just wants to find out what is wrong with the vehicle, tell him there will be a minimum charge for that kind of work (whatever you think is reasonable based on your estimate of how long the diagnosis will take.)

You should have the normal tools for working on a car, such as socket and drive sets, air tools with an air compressor, plenty of wrenches, jacks, ramps, safety stands, etc. Some cars require metric tools, so you should be aware of that. You should only jack up a car on a stable solid surface, such as a poured concrete pad or driveway for safe work. Always use your safety stands, properly placed under the car, when you are going to work underneath the car. An engine hoist is necessary if you plan to pull or replace the engine of the vehicle. Be sure to follow the business practices listed in the Appendix. One possible problem with this business is that you may not be able to operate this business in certain neighborhoods that have covenants against this kind of work.

Check on the covenants for your neighborhood before you start this business. In order to be competitive with other mechanics, garages, and dealerships, you will have to charge a little less than the brick and mortar businesses. As with any other business, you should treat your customers fairly and do a good job if you want to get jobs to work on.

See the Appendix for normal business practices you should observe.

5. Buy and Fix Cars for Re-sale

Related to the above described 'Backyard Mechanics' business, if you could handle a business like that, you may want to consider a business where you buy used cars, fix them and then re-sell them for a good profit. In some states, an individual can only sell a fixed number of cars each year, without getting a dealer's license. A dealer's license would enable you to sell an unlimited number of vehicles, and to attend wholesale automobile auctions where you can buy cars at much lower prices than you would pay an individual or at a used car dealer. But always be on the lookout for cars sold by individuals that are really diamonds in the rough. Maybe you might find a 60's era muscle car or some other antique, or rare, car that you would not find at a wholesale auction or at a dealer. A good source now is the internet where you can find thousands of cars for sale and search for exactly the make, year, and model you are looking for.

From a car's serial number you can get a Carfax report. It will cost you about $25 per car. The report will tell you if a car (for which Carfax has the serial number is in their data base) has been involved in an accident or not. If a car has been in an accident, the value is going to be very low and it will not be worth your time to repair it and resell it. Note that some cars and trucks, that have been in an accident and have been 'repaired', may not have been repaired correctly, and the car may not be safe to drive.

You don't want to be sued for selling someone an un-safe automobile or truck. In general, you cannot get a Carfax report on very old or antique cars, unless the vehicle has been involved in a recent accident. Be sure to follow all of the tag and license laws for the state in which you are conducting this business. See the appendix for general business requirements.

If things go well for you, it may be possible to open a brick and mortar business, where classic cars are restored for individuals. There is a good profit in this business, if operated efficiently. But you will have to have a crew of skilled people and a lot of expensive equipment to operate this kind of business. You will also have a significant overhead cost for the building, facilities, and maintenance.

You don't have to have a fancy location in a swanky neighborhood. An ordinary steel building in an industrial area will be fine. People who want their vehicles re-stored will find you. You would most likely have to borrow a significant sum of money from a bank or individual to start a restoration business. Check the Appendix for general business requirements.

6. Buy a car in the South, Sell in the North

This business is a relatively simple business. Basically you purchase a car in the southern states and then you sell to someone in a northern state for a higher price, without doing any fix-up work, except maybe a good cleaning and detailing of the car. Why can you sell the car for a higher price up north? A very simple reason. Most northern states put salt on their streets in the winter time. When a car gets a few years old, it will start to rust, and most older cars up north have rust, unless they have been kept in the garage all the time. There are two ways to do this. You can advertise in northern states that you have a SOUTHERN CAR for sale.
Offer to deliver for an extra charge, or the customer can pick it up where you are, saving the work of delivery. Another way to do it if you have a really hot popular model is to drive it up north, get a motel room and stay there until you sell it. Advertise it in the local newspaper.

I once sold a 1969 Pontiac Firebird within three days with this method. Be sure to follow all the laws covering car tags and license requirements of the state you are operating in. Also use the Internet and target northern states with your ad. Follow the standard business requirements in the Appendix.

7. Start a Sell-Your-Own Car Lot

This is a great business with a low overhead cost and great revenue potential. Your initial investment is mainly to rent or buy a cheap lot that is not usable for building any brick and mortar business or any substantial building. But it may be large enough and long enough to park cars, maybe as many as 50 or 100 cars at a time. An example of a good piece of land for this business is a strip of land along a major highway with lots of traffic. It might be a strip of land between a highway and a railroad track, or between a highway and a waterway, where the land is not wide enough for a brick or steel building of any significant size, but it is wide enough to park one or two long lines of cars. You will have to get permission to make a gravel, or even a dirt driveway for access, if none exists. Check on this before you buy or rent the property. Allow only one driveway for both entrance and exit. You don't have to fence the property, but it would be good to have a gate across the driveway that you could close and lock at night to keep cars from entering the lot when you are not there. Block off any other existing possible entrances that a car could use to enter your lot.

You will need a small shack or a parked van that you can use as your office during the day to check people in and out of the lot.

Here is an example of how it would work: Someone would drive their car into the lot and a sign would direct them to your 'office' or your van where you are. If they want to park their car for a few days or a week, you will charge a fee, say $6 or $7, to park their car for up to a week. You would provide them with a pre-printed sticker or a small sign with your logo on it that they place inside a back window of their car or somewhere easily visible from the outside (So you and others know they are an 'approved' vehicle in the lot.) Another angle here is that if they pay an additional $25 or $50 you will have the car checked by a mechanic. If the car is ok, you proved the car with a 'certified car' sticker (but you don't provide any warranty on the car.) As an example of the amount of revenue that such an operation can generate, suppose you charge $6 per week for every car on the lot, and you have 50 cars on the lot on the average. The revenue is then $300 per week! If your lot becomes very popular and you average 100 cars per week, your revenue is $600 per week or up to $1000 per week if you are in a hot area where you could charge as much as $10 per car per week. That amount of money should easily cover any payments you have to make on your lot.

 If you cannot afford to buy the lot, you should write up a professional-looking business plan which gives a good estimate of your revenue per week and your expenses. With a good plan, you should be able to get a loan on the property from someone. Usually financing a lot requires a 50% down payment. You should be able to borrow the down payment some way, if it is not a large sum. Use your credit cards, relatives, or maybe even friends. I do not recommend taking on a partner for seed money, unless you know the person very well and he or she is of very good reputation. Be sure to check zoning requirements on the property before you rent or buy the property. Also be sure to follow the general business requirements of the Appendix.

8. Home/Office Cleaning and Janitorial

This is another relatively simple (but not easy) business. Capital investment for equipment would include some kind of truck to haul your cleaning materials and cleaning equipment. I recommend a van of some kind to protect your equipment and materials from bad weather. You will need a professional grade vacuum cleaner, a carpet steam cleaning, and then the usual buckets, mops, brooms, miscellaneous tools such as plungers, and some basic plumbing tools, such as pipe wrenches, and a snake rooter for unclogging drains. If you can handle the basic everyday cleaning and simple clogged drains you won't have any trouble handling this business. You may need an assistant or two to help with ordinary cleaning. You will also need cleaning materials, and some type of cart to tote cleaning materials and implements. You will need to scout out your jobs. Try to get steady customers and you should do well in this business. The business also has possibilities for expansion and franchising. Be sure to follow the basic business requirements in the Appendix.

9. Carpet Cleaning and Reconditioning

Related to the janitorial business described above is a business that specializes in just carpet cleaning and reconditioning. Cleaning carpets is not as easy as it sounds. You may run into problems like bad stains, loose and rumpled carpets, or extremely dirty carpets. Unless the carpet is worn out or has holes in it, the carpet can usually be restored. If the carpet is basically good there is usually a solution for each problem. There are excellent stain removal products on the market that can work magic on even very bad stains. There are also products that can soak up oily stains. Kitty liter works great on oily stains. A good vacuum job on a carpet to start with, is the first step. Get a good heavy duty vacuum cleaner with a brush that will raise the nap up and suck dirt out, even if the dirt is down deep. Go over the carpet twice to make sure you get it as clean as possible. Otherwise, when you steam clean it, your steamer will get very dirty and cost you a lot of time to clean it out when you are done. Remember time is money.

The faster you can clean and be ready for the next job, the more money you can make. If the carpet is loose, indicated by "rumpling", it needs to be stretched. You can buy a manual carpet stretcher for less than $50, but I recommend a powered stretcher that will cost about $500.

The powered stretcher will save you a lot of work and pay for itself in a short time. Do all the cleaning, especially steam cleaning, before you stretch it, so that you don't have to re-stretch it after steaming. Once the carpet dries it will be clean, and it will be stretched tightly if you have re-tacked it down properly.

If a carpet is too worn or damaged to restore, you can recommend a carpet company to the customer that you know will do a good job of installing new carpet and maybe give you a commission for referring the customer, if you make arrangements with the carpet dealer ahead of time.

Eventually, you may be able to expand your business to include carpet installation on a contract basis with local carpet dealers. The carpet business has a lot of different ways that you can do business, but start with a limited scope until you learn more about the business.

If you are asked to clean an oriental rug, you must be extremely careful. Some oriental rugs are worth thousands of dollars. If you know how to do it right, you could possibly build your business on specializing in oriental rugs. Here are a couple of tips. Do not use the vacuum brush on an oriental rug. It will tear up the fragile fibers. Use the vacuum attachment only.

Vacuum both sides of the rug. Don't use any harsh soaps or anything containing ammonia. If the rug is so dirty you have to wash it, take it to the driveway or garage floor where you can wash it in the flat condition. Use only cool water. In fact, I recommend washing only in water first. Just washing in water and rinsing two or three times may be enough to clean it.

You can tell by how dirty the rinse water is after each rinse. If it does need soap, use a very mild detergent and test it on a small spot on the carpet first to make sure it does not cause the colors to run. The carpet must be hung up to dry. You can get it dry faster by using a wet-dry vacuum cleaner on it before you hang it up. Some people recommend beating an oriental carpet. I don't recommend doing that. It only causes more wear and tear on the carpet.

A good vacuum job two or three times on both sides should be enough to get all the loose dust out of it. You can find a lot more information on-line by just googling 'How to Clean an Oriental Rug'. Also it's a good idea to visit your local oriental rug dealer and see what you can find out about cleaning oriental rugs. A dealer may have some kinds of rug cleaners for sale, but he is likely to charge a high price for them. You can get something just as good at Wal-Mart in all likelihood.

Be sure to follow standard procedures as outlined in the Appendix to set-up your business.

10. Water Pressure Cleaning

If you can afford to buy a water pressure cleaner, and you have a vehicle to carry it in, you can do this business. This business is simple. You will clean sidewalks, driveways, patios, and other concrete surfaces at a home or business. Only do jobs where the customer allows you to use their water tap. Bring at least 100 feet of garden hose with you that will connect to your pressure cleaner and to the outside water tap at a building on the property.

The main problem is to have a strong enough pressure and amount of water flow to clean a certain amount of square feet in a reasonable time. So, get the best pressure cleaner you can afford to buy. Remember it is not just the amount of pressure the cleaner can provide, but also the amount of water flow it can provide also. A cleaner that will produce 3000psi, but will only allow ½ gallon per minute flow rate, is not as good as 1500psi cleaner that can produce 1 ½ gallons per minute.

But you do need some minimum pressure to be able to clean good. Extremely high pressures can actually damage concrete surfaces, so try to find a happy medium that will clean good in a reasonable period of time without doing damage. Don't buy this machine on-line.

Go to a store which has a good selection and look at the machines carefully. If you buy one and do not like it, take it back to the store and get your money back. If you buy one on-line and you don't like it, you may have trouble trying to get your money back. Before you start one, you should read the instruction manual. Some machines require that you start water flowing through the machine before you start it, because otherwise the pressure pump may be damaged. One way to judge the cleaners is to multiply the pressure in psi times the rate of water flow per minute. The cleaner that has the highest value is most likely to be the best one to get (if it is affordable for you.)

You will have to decide what amount of money your time is worth. The cost estimate you give to the customer should be based on how much time you think it will take to do the job the customer wants done. Be sure to add something for driving your truck to and from the location. Be sure to include your fuel cost, and the cost of the cleaning agents. I don't recommend two-cycle engines. Try to get a four-cycle engine in the pressure cleaner. Make sure you follow the standard business requirements as outlined in the Appendix.

11. Pool Cleaning Service

This business requires a lot of knowledge but not a lot of capital investment. You may need to have a special license, and training to get it, but you do not have to have a degree in chemistry. There will be a considerable amount of physical labor and you will have to be knowledgeable on how to take care of a pool.

The pool must be maintained in a state where it is not amenable to the growth of bacteria, but there is not so much chlorine in it that it burns a swimmers eyes, or even lungs. If you have ever been in a pool that was loaded with too much chlorine, you know what I am talking about.

You must study how to maintain a pool, what chemicals to use, and how to test the water to determine what its condition is. You will also need to be able to add the needed chemicals and be able to properly clean the pool when it is needed. I will not tell you how to maintain a swimming pool in this book. However, Google has a lot of information on the subject. Just search the subject 'How to Maintain a Swimming Pool'. One informative site is the following link: http://www.wikihow.com/Properly-Maintain-Swimming-Pool-Water-Chemistry

You will also need tools for pool cleaning, and a swimming pool test kit. Some pit-falls to avoid: 1) cheap chlorine tablets that dissolve quickly possibly causing damage to re-circulation pumps and pool heaters. 2) An incorrect Ph value, meaning the pool is either too acidic or too basic (caustic.) The test kit should be able to determine the Ph value. A neutral value is approximately 7.0. A good site that explains Ph values can be found at the following link: http://www.elmhurst.edu/~chm/vchembook/184ph.html A value either significantly higher, or lower than 7.0 means that the pool water is not properly balanced. 3) Using chemicals that require frequent testing. You don't want to test a pool every day, unless your customer demands it. 4) Not checking the pool often enough which could result in the pool going out of control. If the pool gets out of control, it will be very difficult to correct and you could be in trouble with your customer.

Be aware that some people have "salt water" pools.

The salt water pool uses a totally different chemical treatment than the chlorine sanitized pools. Again, you need to research how to maintain a saltwater pool if you decide to handle them. Not many people have this type of a pool and it may not be worthwhile to handle a salt water pool because there are already people who specialize in that type. You will do better to stay with one type of pool and become an expert in that type.

Generally, the way the business works is that you would sign customers on a contract. The customer would agree to pay for all chemicals and your labor needed to maintain his pool during the swimming season for his area. Also insert a clause in the contract that you are not responsible for swimming accidents that may happen in the pool. It would be a good idea to have a lawyer go over your contract to make sure you contract is valid and would hold up for you in a court of law.

The best areas to have a pool service are those regions where a pool is usable year-round. Then you can have contracts which cover 6 months or even 1 year. Long term contracts guarantee you work regularly and have a monthly income from each customer that you service.

This is another business where you need to look professional. Get a uniform designed for yourself and your helpers, if any. You should have a white panel truck or van with your logo and pool maintenance sign with your name and business phone number on it. You should advertise on-line and in the Yellow Pages, or the equivalent in your area. Be sure to meet the local and state requirements for pool servicing. Follow the general business requirements as given in the Appendix.

12. Mold Removal

This is another low capital, but labor intensive business. The mold removal business basically has three steps. 1) The first step is to find out what degree of removal the customer wants and then make a survey of the premises before you bid on the job. You may not want to take a very bad job where the mold contamination is extensive. Some properties with black mold infestation have to burned down to get rid of it. Don't take any job with that degree of infestation. If you decide to make a bid, get a contract for the removal process and the verification of the results, successful or not, signed by the customer.

Note: Some customers may only need a quick clean-up to pass a visual inspection, and they don't really care if the mold is permanently removed or not. Others may insist on a permanent mold removal and a testing verification process after removal is completed. You bid accordingly.

Be careful if verification is required. Have a clause in your contract that the customer must pay 80% (or some percentage that will cover your costs at least) of the bid cost regardless if the mold removal is not verified to be successful. 2) The mold contamination must be tested in a certified lab and a report detailing the type(s) of mold contamination present on the customer's premises.

A report is issued to the customer along with a copy for yourself. Depending on the results of the initial test, you may need to change your bid, in which case you need to get a new contract with the new bid on it, signed. (The fine print on the original contract allows you to change your bid if necessary after the initial test results are obtained.) 3) After removal is complete, and the customer wants verification of the clean-up results, a second set of samples is collected and lab test is done. The final report is issued to verify that removal is completed successful or not.

You must be knowledgeable in how to clean up and deal with different kinds of molds. Also be aware that some molds are toxic to humans and precautions such as protective gear for workers should be provided. Protective clothing would include full head protection, face masks with canister breathing filters for biological materials, haz-mat suits, gloves, and foot covers.

Make sure that you have a bold warning on your worker's contracts that their work could expose them to toxic materials and by signing the contract they absolve you of any fault due to exposure, accidental or otherwise, to the toxic materials (get a lawyer to check your contract and change the wording as he or she directs.)

You should have an arrangement with a good testing lab that can analyze samples and provide you a report at a reasonable cost. Of course, the customer pays for the tests as well as the removal work.

It is best to collect the samples with an impartial witness who can certify that the samples were collected in an impartial and random manner.

You will do best by hiring contract labor to do the work, while you look for more jobs to bid on and get set-up. Clean-up materials will usually consist of items like bleach, ammonia, and soap and water. Tools will usually consist of stiff brushes, scrapers, mops, etc.

Another service you can provide is to paint the surfaces that you have cleaned once they have dried out. Of course, this will be an extra charge on the contract. Note however that if the surface is not completely free of mold, painting the surface will not, in general, be successful.

But painting will give you an advantage in that it will be hard to detect small residues that may have been missed during clean-up work. To look professional you should have some kind of truck or vehicle that you can advertise your business name, logo, telephone number, and your website if you have one. It would be good to get on Angie's List for this kind of work. You can obtain a 'mildew resistant' paint that will help provide longevity of the paint job. Follow all of the general business requirements as outlined in the Appendix.

13. Pest Removal (Varmints)

In the animal pest removal business you will basically remove varmints from homes and businesses. The pests will be miscellaneous small animals such as rats, mice, squirrels, chipmunks, snakes, bats, bird nests, and other pests except insects. Removal of and treatment for insects is a totally different business, and we will treat that separately.

The varmint removal business is a low tech business but it will require skills such as baiting and setting traps, catching varmints on the run, and possibly cleaning up nasty messes varmints can leave, such as bat dung, or other nasty deposits.

Before you agree to do a job, make sure you survey the premises. If the customer refuses to let you take a look in advance, don't take the job. If the job seems overwhelming to you, don't take that job either because you may not be successful in the removal.

Be sure your contract covers all kinds of contingencies such as inadvertent damage to the premises during the removal process. If you are not successful in the removal process, don't charge the customer. You don't want to get a bad reputation.

On the other hand, if you are successful, charge the full price you quoted, or less depending on how difficult the job is, and how much removal you accomplished. You may have to make several visits to flush out all of the pests. A lot of varmints will just move right back in again after a removal. So frequent removal is usually required. Make sure the customer understands these facts ahead of time. Therefore you should try to get the customer on a contract for a monthly inspection and removal, if necessary, covering at least a year's work. The more contracts for monthly service you can get, the more steady your business will be.

The price for varmint removal can be quite high as you usually will not have a lot of competition in this type of business. You should quote at least $500 for a single job that you think might be difficult. You can always reduce the charge if the work turns out to not be difficult. For a year's contract you could charge probably $30 per month, or $360 for a year. To look professional you should have a panel truck or van painted with your business name, logo, telephone number, and website address if you have one. It would also be good to be on Angie's list if you can afford it.

Be sure to follow the general business requirements as outlined in the Appendix.

14. Pest Removal, Insects

This business is more complex than the rodent removal business. You must have or develop a lot of knowledge about insects and the various pesticides that will work to eradicate each type of pest. The main thing about this business is that of protecting against termite infestation and certifying that the property has been and will be guaranteed to be free of termites for a certain number of years.

Usually the customer is signed to a yearly contract which authorizes you do a monthly inspection for termites, and charge for each inspection. Some companies place a piece of wood in a container set into the ground. I will not go into details, but one warning that I will give you is that when you have certified a property to be termite free, you better watch it closely, because if it does become infested, your company will be liable for damages. So you will need special insurance to cover that liability in such an event. Otherwise the business is lucrative when operated efficiently.

You should try to get as many yearly contracts as you can on monthly payments to have a steady income. I will not go into a lot of other details. The main business is roaches and termites. One other caution, however is that you should protect yourself from the hazardous chemicals while you are working.

A dangerous job request my involve removing a hornet nest. You may not want to take such a job as it is very dangerous unless you have special clothing, gloves, and a covering for you head, etc. You will probably not have a lot of calls for that anyway. One thing that you should have in this business is a panel truck or van with you business name, logo, telephone number, and a website address if you have one.

Websites are good to have especially if you can reach local people. Angie's list is also good to be on if you can qualify and afford to be listed. One other thing is that certain regions are better for this business than others. For example, there is not much call for insect removal in Canada in the wintertime, but there is a year-round problem with termites in New Orleans, USA.

Be sure to follow the general business requirements in the Appendix.

15. Computer Systems Network Set-up and Repair

This business is only good for you if you have computer and information technology knowledge and the ability to do the work. It is not something you can learn overnight. On the other hand you do not need a college degree either.

Most of the time it is just a matter of finding a faulty circuit board or a bad network terminal and replacing said unit. Sometimes you will need to install some coax cables if you are setting up a network for a business, but most of the time it will just be Wi-Fi or Ethernet.

Doing work for a doctor's office is usually good and rewarding work, because doctors are not usually computer savvy and they will need help often. Of course you charge by the hour only on a contract basis. Be prepared for a lot of 'My computer does not work' calls. It is usually just a matter of re-booting the computer. If a computer

is running too slow it usually just needs a
cleaning using a software package.
There some good ones that can be downloaded
for free. I use PC Clean, Microsoft Security
Essentials, and Advanced System Care. All of
these packages are free and can be downloaded
on site for any computer. Of these, I use
Advanced System Care to do 'Deep Cleaning'
every day or two. You can do it on a customer's
computer on site. Of course you can also sell the
customer on expanding his computer memory.
You then order the extra memory and install it
for the customer.

And don't forget that you should be ready to
recommend that the customer buy a new
computer or Ethernet system, if he or she really
needs one. If so, you should have a wholesale or
a low price source for obtaining computers and
network equipment.
I recommend Dell computers as they are
generally high quality and long lasting machines.
One other thing you need for this business to
look professional, is a panel truck or van with
your business name, logo, telephone number, and
website address if you have one.
It is also a good idea to be listed on Angie's list if
you can afford it. I won't go into any more
details about this business. You yourself will
know if this business is for you or not.
If it is, also be sure to check the general business
requirements in the Appendix.

16. Business/Technical Consulting

Business and Technical consulting is for people who have a specialized knowledge of some area of business or some field of technology. It does not necessarily require a college degree. For example, a retired military person may have extensive knowledge of missiles or some other kind of military hardware. These people are in demand by certain military contractors, and even certain military bases that need such personnel for R&D work. Another example would be a reformed computer 'hacker' who wants to go straight. The National Security Agency actually advertises jobs for these people, if they qualify of course.

Almost any business or technical enterprise is a possible customer for someone who has specialized knowledge in some area of expertise. Maybe you have some kind of special business or technical knowledge that you could market as a consultant. There are probably a lot of people who have such knowledge and don't realize that they could make good incomes as a consultant. There are two main ways that a consultant gets work. 1) By becoming known by his peers as an expert in his field. He can contact friends and acquaintances and let it be known that he or she is available to contract as a consultant. In this mode of operation, business arrangements are usually rather informal.

Typically, on a request from a person representing some company or organization, the consultant will provide an estimate of the time required to complete the task, and quote a certain amount of money he or she will charge per hour. Contracts in this mode are usually short ones, a few days, or a few weeks at the most. The company or organization will ask the consultant to fill out a W2 form so that the earnings can be reported to the government as an expense for the organization.

 Of course the consultant will be responsible to report his income from the job on his tax return. As in normal business, the consultant will submit an invoice to the organization once the work is done and the consultant has submitted a suitable report on the work done. When submitting your report, remember to be diplomatic if the results may have a negative impact on the organization. But don't gloss over problems either.

 Be careful to put disclaimers in your report that by acceptance of your report, the organization will not hold you responsible for any problems caused by your work. This may not be enough to protect you in some situations, so you still need a good business liability insurance policy. 2) The second method is to work through a contracting agency where you make yourself available for short or long term assignments. Note that you may have to be available to travel almost anywhere to do assignments. Get your passport in order. In this method, you will usually work for a certain amount of money per hour until the work is done and the contract is finished. Usually, the organization contracting you will give you a one-way ticket to the job site, but after that you pay your own expenses and your own transportation back home.

Some companies may give you a per diem expense allowance, but if they do, you will probably get less money per hour also. Be sure you get enough of a job description to determine whether or not you really want the job and believe that you can really do the job successfully. Find out ahead of time if you should bring your own computer or if you are required to use the organization's computers. Some military contractors or sites do not allow personal computers to be brought to the job site. Of course, your contracting agency gets a cut of your pay as their fee. Don't forget to estimate all of your expenses at the remote location, such as a rental car, hotel room, food, and laundry.

Find out if you will need any special gear, clothes, shoes, etc., that the organization does not provide to you. Be sure to follow the general business requirements in the Appendix.

17. General Contracting, Home Repairs, Remodeling

In the business of general contracting in the building trades, you could do anything from very small jobs at a customer's home to building an entire home, or even doing some kind of major work for an industrial company. One way to get started is to just do small jobs by yourself, such as painting a house, installing new doors, windows, etc. You may do small installation jobs for Lowe's or Home Depot.

Maybe you will develop expertise in some area, such as kitchen cabinet installation, countertop refinishing, solid countertop installation (granite, etc.), and tile work. You could also do flooring repair, install carpeting, hardwood floors, etc.

As your skill and business expands, you may need to hire one or more persons to help you. If you do, remember to hire them only on a contract basis, not as an employee. Some jobs you do may require the services of a concrete crew, an electrician, or a plumber. Find some good people for the jobs you contract out.

You are a contractor, not an employer. If you do grow your business, you will eventually need one or more vehicles, depending on how many people you transport to the job site, what kind of materials you haul, and what kind of business you are doing. You may need a heavy duty truck for daily use, but in the case of large equipment such as a bulldozer, crane, or other equipment that you do not use everyday, it should be leased or rented, not purchased.

You can write off all rentals or leases of equipment as a direct expense on you business income tax return, whereas equipment owned must be kept on your books and assigned a depreciation schedule set up by your accountant. You should have at least one panel truck or van, with your business name, logo, telephone number, and website displayed in large print on the back and sides of the vehicle.

You will need some hand and power tools, but only buy enough to do your work. Don't go overboard on buying equipment or expensive power tools you might never even use. It would be good to be listed with the Better Business Bureau and 'reputation' checking sites such as Angie's List.

Also, there are people who will only hire someone that is listed in the 'Yellow Pages'. Don't forget to be bonded and insured. This is explained in the Appendix. Be sure to follow the general business requirements outlined in the Appendix.

18. Illustrator

If you are good at sketching or drawing, you may be able to get contracts, or even a permanent job, as an illustrator. There is a need for commercial artists who can quickly make professional looking drawings of the human figure and other subjects. Possible markets for this work are newspapers, magazines, catalog printers, and any media that uses the process of printing information and drawn images on paper, and websites that have catalog pages or other content with drawn images, animation, etc.

Animation work may require a knowledge of software to produce moving images, and to produce the images in the first place. A cartoon of animated characters telling a short commercial message is an example. Be aware that animation work is difficult and requires a high degree of creativity.

A good example of a single drawing contract, is a job for an author who has written a book and needs someone to prepare a good-looking cover for his or her book. This work is available both for printed books and for electronic books such as on Kindle, Nook, etc. Here is a typical website that is an example of a way to get freelance work (of almost any type):

http://www.ifreelance.com/?gclid=CL3tsuHCwa 8CFQXqnAodhVt8wQ

You will know before you get into the illustration freelance business whether or not you are a good enough artist to do this work. You should have some talent for art, but you can usually find an art or drawing class, somewhere in your local area, where you can get some basic instruction in illustration. Be sure to follow the general business requirements as given in the Appendix.

19. Deliver Newspapers

Delivering newspapers sounds like a lowly job, but it can be an excellent source of part-time income when you need it. There can be more to the business than appears on the surface. For example, there are several nationally distributed newspapers that are home delivered to subscribers in a lot of localities. If you were able to deliver several newspapers each day, the money could be quite significant for you. In my local area there are at least three different national newspapers that are home delivered. These are the Wall Street Journal, USA Today, and Investors Business Daily. All three of these subscriptions are relatively expensive so the fees you earn by delivering them can be substantial. It may be a little difficult to keep track of what home gets what newspaper, but after a while you will learn the route and it will not be difficult. By the way, if the weather is bad, make sure the double-bag the newspapers so that they do not get wet before the customer can get the paper. You don't want your customers to get mad at you and making you deliver them another copy, or worse, cancel their subscription and report you to the newspaper main office. Make sure you deliver the newspapers before people start leaving for work. A good time to deliver is about 4AM to make sure customers will get their paper before they leave for work. Otherwise, the business is like most other businesses. Be sure to follow the general business requirements listed in the Appendix.

20. Airport Shuttle Service

All you need for this business is a dependable mini-van or passenger van. The business consists of transporting people from the airport to their hotels or homes in town, and transporting people from the hotels or their homes to the airport. Depending on the situation in your locality, you will need a chauffer's license, and a permit or license to operate to and from the airport. Someone else will already have a license to do this before you even get started, so one question for you to research, is whether or not the airport rules will allow more than one service like this. It is more likely that a big city will allow more than one shuttle service to operate.

Alternatively, you may be able to contract with a large hotel to act as their shuttle service, if the hotel wants to operate that way (you will need to prove to the hotel that you can save them money by taking care of this service for them.)

In your shuttle service business, you will also have competition from taxi cabs. To deal with this, you will charge a cheaper rate than taxi cabs per person. Why? Because you have an eight passenger van and can make more total money on each trip than a single cab fare will provide to the cab company.

You will do better at a large busy airport than at a small city airport. One important factor in this business is that you should be allowed to set up a booth in the airport where an assistant working for you (under contract) will sell tickets for a ride on your shuttle. Your service should be prominently advertised on your booth and on your van, with your business name, logo, telephone number, and website, if you have one. But don't advertise your price per person.

A traveler must enquire for your rate at the booth or by advance telephone reservation. Be careful not to give your rate to anyone but a legitimate traveler. You can verify that a traveler is legitimate by enquiring what airline and flight number he or she is arriving on or leaving on. Then you can verify on your computer whether or not the passenger has a reservation, or not, if you can obtain this information on your computer (you will have to get permission from the airlines that operate out of the airport to access their passenger reservation records.)

At least you should be able to verify that the flight number and the time of arrival or departure the traveler gives you is a valid flight number, or not. If he or she is not legitimate, do not reveal your rate. You don't want a competing service to undercut you by finding out what your rate is, and charging a lower price than you are. Of course you have to take into account all of your expenses, such as gasoline and service on your vehicle.

You should obtain a vehicle that is new, or relatively new, so that it will be dependable and make a good appearance. It might be best when you are starting out to buy a vehicle that is one or two years old, until you know for sure you have a viable business, or not. If the business is not working out, you can then sell the vehicle and get some of your money back.

Once you have a going business and have confidence that your business will remain good, it would be better to lease a new vehicle with a good warranty. Lease terms can be negotiated, so try to get the best lease possible with a full warranty on the vehicle that will take care of all service expenses, except consumables like tires, batteries, oil changes, and engine belts. If you can operate your business efficiently, it should be a very good steady business with a good income. Be sure to follow the business requirements in the Appendix.

21. Same Day Local Package Delivery Service

This business is viable if there is a market in your local area for a fast low cost letter or package delivery service. It would most likely be delivery between businesses, or rapid delivery to a flight for air transport. This service is more likely to work in a large city with lots of business activity. A small van should be all that you will need to get started. You don't want a very large vehicle that will be difficult to park in the city. Be careful that you do not deliver any drugs or illegal commodities.

Deal only with reputable establishments or people. You should have a clear written description of where you are to deliver an item (if you are not sure of the delivery location), and make sure you get the person receiving the item to sign for it so that you can prove that you did deliver the item successfully.

If you cannot make a signed legitimate delivery, take the item back to who gave it to you to deliver. Never just leave an item on a doorstep. Make sure you keep good records of who you received an item from to deliver.

Record the time and date when you receive the item, when you made the delivery, and to whom (with a signature.) You must decide how you want to get paid. If you are not sure if a certain company or person will pay you after you have made a delivery, you should require money up-front for the delivery at the start.

However, if you have a steady customer with a good reputation, you may bill the customer monthly, giving the customer 30 days to pay their bill. Most companies you deal with would rather pay you in that way with a check in the mail, instead of having to hand you money for each delivery. Most companies will not want to give you cash every time you make a deliver something for them.

If you are dealing with an individual, you should get money in advance for the delivery. Some customers will want to have their item insured. Of course you charge extra for that service and give them a chit that shows how much their item is insured for. Be careful. Don't allow the customer to make you insure for a large amount, for example over $1000 or whatever maximum amount you are comfortable with.

The 'customer' could be trying to hit you with a big claim in a scam set-up. Make sure your liability insurance will cover large losses. You will have to absorb small losses out of your own pocket as your liability insurance will most likely have a 'deductable' amount of $500 or $1000. This is another reason to keep good records and make sure that the person who signs for the delivery is really entitled to receive the delivery and gives you a proper signature.

Sometimes a person will just scribble some initials or his signature is illegible. So what you should do in all cases is make the person who is receiving the item, print his name under his signature.

If you can deliver items quickly and accurately with high efficiency, you may have a viable business. But you should realize that this business is far more difficult than it would seem at first glance and will require careful analysis and research before you start such a business. Be sure to follow the business requirements in the Appendix.

22. Moving and Storage

You should have a large box van, but it does not have to be a shiny new one. It should be dependable so that you do not have to spend a lot of time and money repairing it. One important thing about a moving van is that it should be clearly marked with your business name, telephone number, and website address if you have one. If you can purchase one, or already have a large van, you have a possibility of starting a moving business. You will most likely start with local house-to-house moves first, before you attempt doing national moving. You will need to contract at least one assistant to help you move goods. You cannot do it all by yourself. It helps if you are big and strong. Your assistant should also be big and strong. Make sure you check out people before you contract them. It is a high level of temptation to pilfer items from a house when moving furniture and goods. You don't want someone stealing customer's items. It will be very bad for business. You can check out people to see if they have a police record, and you should also get references on anyone before you contract them. There are a number of sites that you can find to do background checks. You will most likely have to pay for it. Here is one site to get you started:

http://www.ussearch.com/

To get started you need to do some research to determine how much competition you will have in your operating area. Also try to find out what the lowest moving rates are that your competition is quoting. You could find this out by calling movers and asking them for a quote to move your furniture across town or somewhere. Once you know what the lowest rates in your area are, you should start your business with rates that are slightly lower than the lowest rate you have found.

Once your business is going and growing, you may be able to raise your prices some. You need to find a rate level that provides the customer an attractive rate, while still making a profitable business for you.

So what about the storage part of the business? Well if you were to attempt to buy or lease a warehouse suitable for storing customer's goods, it would be a very expensive proposition. There is an alternative, and that is to use an existing storage complex owned by someone else.

You will do some enquires to find the lowest storage cost business with reasonable secure facilities, and arrange with the owner to store your customer's goods at his establishment. If you have enough business with the storage company, the owner might give you a discounted rate. The customer will pay you to store his goods and you will pay the storage company to rent the space for your customer, and then move the goods to be stored to that storage location and locker. You may also have to arrange for temperature controlled storage for sensitive items such as antiques and electronic components. Of course you will charge your customer a little more than the storage company charges you, to cover your expenses and insurance on the customer's goods.

You should make a small profit on the storage of your customer's goods each month. In your storage contract you will have a clause that if your customer does not pay his storage bill within 15 days (or whatever is allowed by your local laws), you automatically take possession of the customer's goods.

Make sure the customer knows about the 15 day requirement. Of course you will have to pay the storage company so that you can pick up the goods. Your other option is to let the storage company take possession of the goods, if you think the goods are not of enough value to sell.

Your customer does not need to know where you store their goods but if they ask tell them you have a special arrangement with the storage company and you insure their goods.

If the customer objects, tell them that you will transport their goods to any storage location they might choose, but they will have to make their own arrangements and you will not insure their goods if they choose their own storage location. They may change their mind or they may not, but remember, the customer is always right.

By the way some people may want to store their goods at some very high rate of insurance. Give them a maximum amount that you and your insurance company are comfortable with. Be careful here.

Someone may be trying to do a scam by insuring their goods at a high rate and then the goods mysteriously disappear. Don't give the customer access to their storage bin without your presence. You keep the keys or access card under your control. I will not go into any more details on this business. Be sure you follow the general business requirements in the Appendix.

23. Resume Writing

If you have some business experience and you are a good fast typist, you may be able to prepare resumes for people. There is plenty of information on the web that tells how to write a good resume. Note that the format of resumes that are considered 'good', changes with the years, just like fashions change.
So you need to find up-to-date examples of good resume formats and use the best in your work.
Usually you would charge a flat fee for creating a resume for someone, for example $25 for simple one page resumes, and $50 for complicated resumes (usually a well written one-page resume is the most effective.)
The hardest part of this business is finding out the facts from the customer concerning his or her job objectives, education, experience, publications, hobbies, and so forth.
A resume needs to be clear, concise, and cover pertinent information concerning education and job experience. Time periods for each job should

be given and there should be no missing time, or periods where there is no explanation for not having a job.

Advise the customer that you will not be responsible for any falsehoods in the information that he or she gives you. Make the customer sign your terms and conditions form so that he or she agrees that you are not responsible for inaccuracies or falsehoods on the resume.

After you have written a resume, check it carefully for typographical errors or omissions. When you are satisfied, make a copy that is usable for proof reading only (so the customer cannot just take the copy and disappear, not paying you anything.)

The easiest way to do this is to give the customer a proof copy that is triple spaced so that it could not be used for reproduction and use. Then make the customer proof-read it. Make any corrections that are needed and make the customer proof-read it again.

When the customer is satisfied with your work make him or her sign your acceptance form and get full payment before you let the customer have the final version and any copies he or she wants. It is best to do everything on hard copy and deal face-to-face with the customer. For distant customers, email copies are the second choice to use. To make the email version of the proof copy it should be overprinted with large grey words such as 'proof only' or 'preliminary'. You can do this with Microsoft Word or use other means such as printing on pre-marked paper and then scanning the result for the emailed proof copy. One other piece of advice:

If the customer wants his copies printed on some kind of fancy heavy bond or colored paper, try to talk him or her out of that request because those kinds of resumes are the first to go into the trash basket. I won't go into more detail on this business.

It is a relatively simple business if you are good at typing and you have a computer with a good printer such as a laser printer. I don't recommend ink-jet printers. Be sure to follow the general business requirements as given in the Appendix.

24. 'Find a Job' Counseling

You don't need a doctor's degree or a Masters in Business Administration (MBA) in this business. All you need is some good knowledge and experience in looking for a job and landing the job. You should also be a good communicator, able to talk to people one-on-one, and speak confidently to a group of people. This business is a step up from the resume writing business, but you will also provide resume preparation help to your customers as described above.

You should have some salesmanship ability for this kind of work. It is really a marketing job. You are marketing your experience and knowledge to a group of people that you are capable of helping.

The group you will market your skills to depends on what kind of jobs you have had and what experience you have. For example, if you are a retired executive, you might market to the retired executives that are looking for work. Or you may have an engineering or information technology background so you would market your skills to that group.

You need to do some advertising.

First talk to your friends and contacts and tell them you are starting the job counseling business and ask them to help you spread the word. to give them an incentive you might pay them some money for each person they refer to you that signs up for your counseling service.

You might also try advertising in your local newspaper. For example, your ad might read: "Need a job? Free seminar Tues. night 7PM. Call 123-4567 for reservations. Limited space." You will have to arrange for a room somewhere. Usually, large local hotels will rent you an empty conference room for an evening. I have done this myself with good to excellent results.

As your business grows, you only need to keep your name and telephone number in the minds of people. For example, you might have a billboard advertisement: "Michael Crawlforth Job Counselors, Tel. 123-4567, yourwebsite.com". (You should also have a website for this business.)

Using Social Networks. You can place advertisements for almost any business on the social networks, such as Facebook, at reasonable rates. I regularly post advertisements on Facebook directly into the stream at no cost. So far only one person complained. I explained to him that I was a small businessman and that Facebook has no rule against it (as long as you don't abuse the use of it for unpaid ads.) He replied back to me that it was ok to post my messages. Lately I have seen companies advertise in-stream just like you would post a message to Grandmother.

By the way there are three ways to build an audience on Facebook: 1) Find people that you know and request them to be friends with you. 2) Join groups that have an interest that fits with your business, such as business groups. Some groups have as many as 10,000 people as members. 3)

Subscribe to people under the 'Subscribe' list using the 'see all' link. Some of the people you subscribe to will subscribe you back. You can build up thousands of subscribers this way. Between your friends, groups you belong to, and people that subscribe to you, you can reach thousands of people with each post you make.

Another good social network is Google Plus. It is possible to accumulate thousands of people in your 'circles' fairly quickly if you work at it.

Another good social network is Twitter. All kinds of messages are posted on Twitter and many of them are business messages so this is a site you can really post a lot of business messages.

You build followers on Twitter by 're-tweeting' other people's messages. The more posts and re-tweets you do every day, the more followers you will build up. Also there are free online classified ad websites where you can place classified ads for as long as 6 months at a time.

 I won't go into any more detail on the job counseling business but be sure to read the general business requirements in the Appendix.

25. Mentoring/Tutoring

This business category covers a wide range of work, from tutoring school children in arithmetic to mentoring executives in business or government jobs. The category you select depends on your knowledge, education, and experience. For example, maybe you were a school teacher who taught elementary algebra. That would be a great subject to tutor in because a lot of students have trouble with algebra.

Or maybe you have a lot of experience in stock investments so you could be an investment counselor or mentor. Maybe you are a musician skilled in some instrument such as a saxophone. Then you could teach the saxophone to students who have signed up for band practice or just someone who wants to play the saxophone. It could be any instrument such as piano, trumpet, guitar, and so forth. Or maybe you are a retired executive with years of experience learned the hard way. You would then be in a position to mentor other executives who want to make the right decisions in their career. Any field of work that you have become an expert in, or you are highly skilled in, is an opportunity for you to start mentoring others. Of course you will charge your customers according to what your time is worth and what the market will allow.

Like any other business, you should be competitive on your fees with other similar services. To get this business started, you should talk to all your friends and contacts and tell them you are going into the mentoring or tutoring business and what field you are specializing in. You might pay your friends a bounty for each person that they refer to you that signs up for your service.

Small ads in your local newspaper should help you get customers. You should have a website that gives your experience profile and describes your service, whatever it is, and information on how to contact you.

You should know right away what field or fields you could tutor or mentor in. I will not go into any more detail on this business but you should read the general business requirements in the Appendix.

26. Business Guidance/Consulting

If you have a lot of business experience in some business area, such as marketing, operations, accounting, human relations, information technology, engineering, and so forth, you may be in a position to provide business guidance or consulting services. You may want to provide only guidance to people who are trying to start a business.

This type of business activity is related to the mentoring business described above.

On the other hand, if you are doing the consulting work, you will be trying to solve a business problem someone is having at some company or organization. You may need to travel to the business location to provide the help that is needed.

You would charge the customer for your travel and other expenses related to the job plus your hourly fee for the work.

Consulting work is more difficult and also has some risks associated with the work. For example, if you suggested a solution to a problem and your solution did not work, or it actually caused some kind of damage, you could be subject to a lawsuit and payment for damages as well punitive damages to you.

So you must have good liability insurance for this kind of work. It would also be wise to incorporate your business as a limited liability corporation (LLC) or an S-corporation both of which protect you to a limited extent from damage liabilities.

You will immediately know what kind of guidance or consulting work you can do. As above, start with contacting your friends about your new business. The consulting work has possibilities for expansion.

For example, you could partner with other experienced business people or consultants and keep building your business possibly into a large business.

If you want to advertise, you can use the social networks as described above, start a blog, or maybe even advertise on a billboard. I will not go into a lot of other details on this business. Be sure to follow the general business requirements of the Appendix.

27. Start an On-Line Store

Instead of creating a 'brick and mortar' store, which is the old-fashioned way to do business, why not start an on-line store? If you know of something you can make or buy at a whole-sale price, and there is a good market to re-sell it at a good profit, then you have a possibility of starting an on-line store.

A simple example is coffee. If you know where you can buy quality coffee at a whole-sale price, it would be a good product to sell on line as there is a substantial market for quality coffees. But you always need to research your marketing prospects on any item you think you can sell.

There are some things you need to know first, such as how much competition will you have? What is a competitive price you could sell at and still make a profit? What do you estimate your sales and profits will be in the first year? Can you maintain the business long enough until you start making a profit, or will it take too long and take too much of your money to make it work?

Have you found enough good sources for your product, or can you produce enough product to satisfy your customers? Can you find a secure way to process credit cards? Where can you get the special software required? There are no doubt, a lot of other questions to be answered depending on the type of store you want to set-up and the kind of products you want to sell.

But what if you don't have a product that you can produce or find to sell? There are a lot of drop-ship companies that you can make arrangements with to sell their products and they will ship the products directly to the customer. You only do the marketing and collect the customer payments. Of course you have to pay the drop-shipper his portion of the price you charged the customer.

If setting up the store all by yourself is overwhelming to you, you may use the services of a company that will help you set up your store. I don't necessarily recommend any particular service, but a good example of such a company is Volusion. The link is:

http://www.volusion.com

Volusion partners with a drop shipper and you can sell hundreds of products or even thousands. They provide you tools to set-up your store including a secure way to process credit cards. If you already have a large supply of some type of item you would like to sell, such as DVDs, CDs, books, or even LP records, for example, you could partner with Amazon.com or Ebay.com to set-up an on-line presence for your store. Both of these companies will take care of the credit card stuff so it greatly simplifies the set-up for you. The main thing I like about an on-line store is that it is a modern method of retailing that is not limited by the inconvenience of 'brick and mortar' stores.

It is so easy to order on-line and most of the time orders are quickly delivered, sometimes without shipping charges. If you are at a rural location or somewhere that is distant from large brick and mortar stores, you may have to drive a long distance to get to the store, and then the store may not even have the item you are looking for. I know I used to drive all over town to different stores and not find the item I was looking for. Now I will search for an item on-line and usually find what I am looking for. I place my order and get the item usually within a few days. Some companies that I deal with, will send me an email, alerting me about special sales that they have on the kind of products I usually buy.

So if you do an online store, try to get a customer's email address so you can periodically contact the customer about sales you have or new product information. Your website should have a feature that allows the customer to register with his email and a password so he can log into your site and you will know who is accessing your site and how frequently.

But don't make a customer register in order to buy something from you. Allow "guests" to buy as well. I will not go into more details on this business, but be sure to review the general business requirements listed in the Appendix.

28. Start a Catalog Business

Starting a catalog business is very similar to starting an on-line store described in business no. 27 above. It may even be a division of your on-line store. The main difference is that older people who do not use a computer sometimes like to do their business by ordering on the telephone or sending in order forms from catalogs.

Of course you will have the expense of printing and mailing a nice color catalog and you need a lot of products to list in your catalog. One way to get started is to use the services of a company that will sell products to you wholesale and also provide you with colorful catalogs that you can send to potential customers. One such company that has been in business a long time is SMC. Here is a link to their website:

http://www.startwithsmc.com/

Be careful. Be sure to carefully evaluate any company you choose to do business with.
You will need a good mailing list to get your business started. You may specialize in a certain type of product such as women's clothes, or some other item that will have a good market. Usually you will take orders over the telephone, so either you will have to answer the phone yourself, or you could contract with some telephone order processing service. Most catalogs also have a website address that the same products or more can be ordered from by the customer.
There are more expenses involved with having a catalog store, so you will need to have great products that sell good and have a good profit margin. You need to do the same market research and answer the same questions about the business that you do for any store before you start this business (refer to business no. 27.) I will not go into more details on this business. Be sure to review the general business requirements listed in the Appendix.

29. Start a Pyramid Sales Business

Yes, pyramid sales marketing really does work if you are willing to put in an effort to do the hard work. This is one of the hardest businesses to operate successfully but the rewards are great if you can create a good 'down-line' organization. Alternatively, you can operate the business at a low level selling part-time to your friends, relatives, and neighbors. What are some of the businesses that you could become a representative for? Some of the more well-know ones are Amway, Herbal Life, Avon, and Mary Kay.

Some are harder to work for then others so be choosy in your selection. It may be possible to represent more than one company at the same time, depending on what restrictions are in each company's terms and conditions.

Be careful. Read the company's terms and conditions carefully before you start with one. Also make sure the company's products are not over-priced and hard to sell. You will have to do a lot of research before you start. You will have to evaluate how many people you know that could be potential customers.

Also, how many people do you know that might be candidates for your 'down-line' sales representatives. When your down-line representatives make sales, you get a percentage of their sales.

Your down-line representatives can also sigh up their representatives, and you also get a percentage of their sales. This is why people use the derogatory phrase "It's a pyramid scheme." Don't let it discourage you. Relatives are sometimes experts in discouraging you from starting a business, no matter what it is. Don't listen to that kind of talk unless someone knows some concrete facts to back up their negative criticism. I won't go into more detail on this business. Be sure to read the general business requirements in the Appendix.

30. Freelance Computer Programmer

In this business you will need to be an expert in all kinds of computer programming. If that is not you, skip this business. But if you have a lot of experience developed on-the-job, maybe working for the same company, or maybe several different companies, and you are tired of working for someone else, you may want to work for yourself as a freelance programmer.

As an expert you can command high fees for your work. It is possible to expand your work into a company by contracting other programmers to help with some of the work. You don't need a brick and mortar building. You can work totally on-line with your associates who are maybe at remote locations from your home. Or you can just do jobs when you want to working from home.

You no longer have to spend an 8 to 5 day, 5 days a week at a boring job. You will need to market your talents though. Let your contacts know you are available for contracting on software projects. Don't spend a lot of money advertising. Your fame or notoriety will spread by word-of-mouth.

But you can sign up with technical recruiting agencies who will call you if they have a contract available that fits your profile. This business is not for someone who needs a steady income to support a large family.

But if you can live with occasional jobs, it will give you freedom to take time off and do the fun things you like to do. You will know if you can do this kind of work on a contract basis. I will not go into more details on this business.

But you should read the general business requirements in the Appendix.

31. Contract Engineer/Technician

This business is similar to the contract programmer described above except that it is for a degreed engineer or highly skilled technician in some specialized technical field. Contract engineers are in demand in all areas because of the shortage of qualified engineers. The contract engineer is usually highly experienced in his field and he is not afraid to tackle tough assignments. It's usually best to sign up with a contract engineering agency that will have contracts in your field of technical work. If you fit the profile for a certain contract, the agency will call you and describe the job to you. You will decide if you want the job or not and if you are interested, you quote what rate per hour you want for the work.

You may be bidding against one or more other engineers for the contract, so if you really want the job you might quote a relatively low rate so you have a better chance of getting the contract. On the other hand if you are not really interested in the job, but you think that you can do the work, you might quote a high rate to make it worth your time and work, if you get the contract.

If you are not a degreed engineer, but you have some highly specialized technical experience, such as a missile technician, you may be in hot demand. Good technicians are also in demand. If you are a good technician and you want to do contract work, you should sign up with an agency that works with technicians as well as engineers.

Typically, if you accept a contract to a distant location, the company will send you a one-way airline ticket to the company's location. You will be responsible for all your expenses while you are working at the location, in most instances. Sometimes the job will have certain 'perks' or things provided to you, such as a vehicle, company housing, and maybe free meals, or a 'per diem' expense stipend.

One example of a situation that will provide some of your needs, is working on an oil rig where your room and board is usually provided.

You will have to pay for your transportation back home after the contract is finished.
Also note that you have to take care of any medical insurance you need and saving for your retirement, because in contract work there is no health insurance or retirement plan provided to you.
I will not go into more details on this work. You will usually know if you are qualified to be a contract engineer or technician. Be sure to read the general business requirements in the Appendix.

32. Make Custom Hand-Crafted Furniture

If you love carpentry and you are skilled in precision woodworking with power tools, you may be able to design and build custom or one-of-a-kind furniture that could not be purchased from Wal-Mart or any furniture store. To do this kind of work you will need certain basic power tools such as a table saw, a rotary mitre saw, a planer, a router, wood lathe, power sanding machines, and other miscellaneous hand and power tools.
You should have a place to work that is dry and temperature controlled. If you are skilled in woodworking, you will already know what you need for tools, or you may already have the necessary tools in your garage, shed, or basement. Maybe all you need is the idea to go

ahead and create some designs to start making furniture.

Don't copy someone else. Your work must be unique and totally original. Sit down and think what you would like to do for your projects, maybe table and chair sets, decorative tables, dressers, carved or laminated wood chairs, or whatever.

One of the problems you should think about ahead of time is how you will market your products and what prices you will charge. Will you build items to order, or will you make whatever you want to and then try to sell it, or maybe you can do both? Once you decide what you want to make, you should make some samples for display and available for your potential customers to examine.

How should you advertise your work for sale? One of the best ways to get people interested in your work is to have a display set up at a home show, and other shows that might be related to your work in your local area. You should have a good web site with high quality pictures of your work.

You do not need a fancy building or a store in a mall. If your potential customers like your work, they will come to your home or wherever you can display your work. It may also be possible to make an arrangement with a local furniture store to display one or two samples of your work if you give them a commission on any sales that result from their referrals.

You may have to pay them a fee each month for using some floor space in their building. Another good way to get attention is to place an ad with a picture of one of your works in a major home furnishings magazine. *Woman's Day Magazine* is one example of a good home furnishings magazine (your customers will be mostly women.)

If you are good at your work and become known for your unique designs and workmanship, you will be able to charge relatively high prices for your items. Get a copy of a woodworking magazine to see what others are doing, but again, create your own unique designs.

I will not go into any more details on this business. Be sure to read the general business requirements in the Appendix.

33. Restore Antiques

Restoring antiques is not easy work but it can be rewarding if you know how to do it properly. The best way to do it is to specialize in one type of antique so that you can learn everything you need to know to properly restore that type of antique. You will need to either have or acquire a lot of knowledge on the type you intend to work on so that you can do it properly without damaging the article and rendering the item virtually worthless. You might specialize in antique weapons, furniture, automobiles, or many other categories.

There are two ways to go. Let's say that you are going to restore furniture. So you might search the countryside or missions for antiques that are diamonds in the rough, just waiting for someone to buy them (hopefully at a low price) and turn them into high dollar sales for you. Or, you might just restore furniture for customers who bring them to your shop for restoration.

You charge them according to the amount of work that is involved, and how much you want to get for your time. The first way you have to "invest" money to make money. The second way, you only need the tools and materials to do the restoration work.

Either way I cannot emphasize too much that you must have detailed knowledge of how to restore without causing the item to be ruined or in worse shape than it was when you started to work on it. When an expert on the type of antique examines the item, he will of course know whether the item has been restored or not, so the only question is: *Was the item properly restored or not?* Before you start doing restoration work for real, you should practice on some junk first to refine your techniques.

I once restored an old console tube radio. A bad problem was two cigarette burns right on the top of the cabinet. How did I fix that problem? Amazingly, all I had to do was use some color crayons that I could fill in and cover the burn marks with, and polish over them.

Crayons can also be used to fill in scratches on furniture. This is just to illustrate that you will need to know some tricks and unusual techniques that you may not be aware of to accomplish restoration work. Where can you find items to buy and work on? Some of the best places I have found are missions that have stores such as, Downtown Rescue Mission, Salvation Army, and Goodwill Industries.

There are probably other ones in your local area. When you buy items from missions, you are also helping to support the charity. Other places are generally out in the country, at farms, in barns, sheds, and attics, etc.

Surprisingly, people sometimes put good furniture out on the curb in front of their home for the trash man to remove. I once found a beautiful wooden chair that was in great shape except the seat cover was a little dirty. That problem was easily rectified and when I was done with it, I had a very attractive chair.

Before you start you should think about what you love and what you would enjoy working on. Whatever that is, it is probably what would be best to work on because you will enjoy working on it. You don't need a fancy building to work in. A garage is fine. You don't need a fancy new truck. An old pick-up truck will do fine for hauling a piece of furniture, for example.

I will not go into more details on this business, but you will know if you want to do this business and whether or not you have the skill and knowledge to do the work. Be sure to follow the general business requirements as given in the Appendix.

34. Start a Coffee Shop

For this business you do need a brick and mortar location, but it could be a little hole in wall store front somewhere. Just make sure it is close to where potential customers are, for example close to a factory, or maybe an old down town section where there may be some doctors or lawyers offices. But find somewhere that is low rent and on the first floor.

People are lazy. They will not climb steps even for a great cup of coffee. If you can find a place on a main street or highway that has a lot of traffic, that is good. But don't be by yourself in an isolated location.

Don't do business in a bad neighborhood or a high crime area. Your shop should have room for your coffee brewing machines and your cash register. You should have the usual counter where the customers will come to order their coffee or whatever you have for them to buy. You might have some stools at your counter so people can sit there at the counter and maybe chat with each other or with you. Some people just want someone to talk to. Others want to sit by their table and not talk to anyone. It would be a good idea to provide free Wi-Fi for customers that want to come in and use their lap top computers or tablet computers while they sip on a cup of coffee.

Give people a free re-fill, but don't let someone tie up a table all day without ordering anything. There should also be enough floor space for a few tables and chairs. Don't make your customers stand up while they drink their coffee. Before you agree to rent or lease a location make sure that it is zoned for the type of business you intend to do.

Ok, suppose you have a good location. What should you serve in your coffee shop. You may have several varieties of coffees and some cold sandwiches and deserts. Keep the food in a cold case that is kept just above 32 degrees Fahrenheit.

The Health Department will most likely check the temperature of the case. The coffee you serve may be hot or iced. You may have the usual Capuchino, Latte, Mocha, , Espresso, etc. Go to another coffee shop to see what kinds of coffee they sell. Stick with well known types of coffee such as Columbian, Arabic, etc.

Don't stock up on too much of exotic coffees, but you may have some small quantities on hand in case someone asks if you have a certain coffee. You will need a few fast coffee makers and an Espresso machine so you have serving speed and flexibility.

Friendly and quick service with good tasting products at competitive prices should be your goal. Check the prices in a popular coffee store. You know which one I am talking about.

The chances are good that you can equal or beat their prices if you work in the store yourself and have a low overhead operation. Try to avoid having any employees, but maybe you have a relative or two that might help you out for a share of the profits. It would be a good idea to have security cameras outside and inside your store. If you are a woman, and in the store by yourself, you should learn how to shoot a gun, and keep one handy under your counter for self-protection. Unfortunately, tough customers is one of the problems inherent in brick and mortar stores, so think carefully before you start whether you are willing to deal with that problem or not.

I will not go into any more detail on this business, but you should carefully read the general business requirements in the Appendix.

35. Art Business/Studio

Are you an artist of some kind? Do you paint, make pottery, sculpt, make patch-work quilts, glass work, or any other kind of artwork? Maybe you can make some income doing so, if you are talented, you are expert in your artwork, and productive as far as being able to produce artwork in quantity.

But maybe you are relatively unknown in your field and nobody seems interested in your artwork. As a part-time artist myself, I can tell you that it is very difficult to sell artwork unless you are known in your field.

So how can you become known and start selling your work? The main way is by showing your work; at art exhibitions, various events that are showcasing local artists, and by getting your artwork displayed in local art shops. Expect it to take time to get to be known. One possible way is to arrange your own exhibition. To do this you will have to rent space temporarily at a hall, place a large advertisement in the local newspaper specifying place, date, time, and directions (free admission), and invite as many friends and acquaintances as you can think of.

Try to make friends with someone rich who might be willing to sponsor you (pay for your exhibitions, or buy your artwork.) If at first you don't succeed, try, try again. It will be a long difficult road, but if your work catches on with the art collectors and the public, the rewards could be great.

An example of a successful artist in his lifetime is Thomas Kinkade. What was the secret of his great success? Two things : He created good if not great that appealed to the average person. He was known as the painter of light because his paintings always had bright light in the pictures. Secondly, he created a mass market for his art by having quality prints made. He made the prints look like originals by dabbing a little paint here and there for highlights.

Once you get your business up and running (you are selling your work), you might set up an art studio somewhere. You will need to be in a high traffic area and preferably in a ritzy or tourist area.

Don't set up shop in some isolated or country setting. Some cities are great places to showcase artwork. St. Augustine Florida is a good example, with a lot of tourist, and a lot of artists showing their work.

Of course, there a lot of other cities around the world also, for example, Paris France, where artists produce and display their works.

I will not go into any more detail on this business. Be sure to read through the general business requirements in the Appendix.

36. Make Gizmos

Do you like to invent gadgets in your garage or basement? Do you think you have a hot idea for a mass-market product? If you have invented something, the first thing you need to do is apply for a patent on the gizmo or maybe a series of patents covering all the aspects and intricacies of your invention.

But that is as far as your patent work needs to go: just do the applications and don't actually go the through the full patent process (because of the expense and time involved) at least until you know your product is successful and you want to fully protect your invention.

Make sure your very first production items are marked 'Patent Applied For'. So how do you get started marketing your invention. It won't be easy. First you will have make samples for show and tell. Once you have a sufficient number of samples available, you can start contacting distributors and other sales outlets to get a marketing organization set up.

Keep in mind that the distributors and sales outlets will want a substantial commission on each sale of your product. To get you marketing organization in tact you will need to set up appointments with people that are distributors or operate sales outlets to show your product. What distributors and sales outlets?

You can find a lot of small independent distributors in on-line directories. You should also try to make arrangements with 'the big guys' like Wal-Mart, Target, Home Shopping Network, and others. This will require a lot of phone calls, letter writing, travel, and expenses. It won't be easy and you will get a lot of rejections. But like the Marines, all you need are a few good men (or organizations.)

Next you will need the use of some manufacturing company that makes gizmos like the one you are trying to sell, unless you can build the product yourself. You will need to make agreements or contracts with the factory that it will be able to deliver your products within a certain time of receipt of your orders and in sufficient quantities.

The factory will require that a certain minimum of quantity is ordered so it will be worth their time to make it. They should also give you a price quotation as a function of the quantity you order.

Once you have solid ground on a source for your product, you are then in a position to give your sales distributors the go-ahead to sell your product. Pricing is critical. The first rule on selling gizmos is that they better not cost more than $19.99, or you won't make a lot of sales. But you still have to make a profit and you have manufacturing costs, commissions, and advertising costs to pay for. So nothing is easy in this kind of business. You need to do your own marketing research to make sure you have a practical and useful product before you start. Be sure to think the whole project through before you tackle a business of this high degree of difficulty.

But don't let your friends or relatives talk you out of it either, if you know that you have a good product. I won't go into any more details on this business. Be sure to read the general business requirements in the Appendix.

37. Become a Notary Public

If you are just looking for a little extra income, or something good to put on your resume for a business job, maybe in a lawyer's office or a bank, you may wish to obtain your license with the locality you live in to be an official notary public. Rules for becoming a notary vary from state-to-state, so you will have to do your own research to find out what is required to obtain your license.

If you become a notary public to make some part time income, you should place a small advertisement in the *Yellow Pages* and your local newspaper. If you make it easy for people to find you, and you spread the word with your friends and relatives, you may bring in enough income to make it worthwhile for you.

There is not much more to tell about this relatively simple business, but make sure you report your extra income on your tax returns and follow the general business requirements in the Appendix.

38. Become a Translator

Do you know at least two languages and are you able to read and speak both fluently? If the answer is yes, you may qualify to be a translator. There are two ways to go in this. You could work for the government or possibly a lawyer, or you could work for yourself as a freelance contract translator. In the later business, you would most likely translate documents such as legal papers, technical papers, or even books.

Who would be your likely customers? Lawyers, companies doing business overseas, publishers, or anyone who needs to translate one or more documents. To get started you may want to place small ads in newspapers, and online at sites such as freelance.com, Facebook, Google, and others. Charge just enough to make it worth your time, but not so much that you get underbid by someone else. In translating documents, your work must be professional with correct grammar, punctuation, and accuracy.

You will know whether or not you can do the work or not. If you can't do this work in an accurate and professional manner, don't even try this business. I will not go into more detail on this business, but be sure to read the general business requirements in the Appendix.

39. Become a Ghost Writer

Some writers like to have someone type their book for them, usually based on notes, a detailed outline, or sometimes by verbal dictation. The writer will expect you to be able to write well with good grammar, spelling, punctuation, and the ability to write good prose and detail that will keep the reader interested. It would work best for you if you have a talent for writing, or maybe you were an English Major in college.

If you are good, you may get a lot of business from one writer who is prolific and well known for his books.

The right person could keep you busy for years. On the other hand you may do a lot of single jobs on a contract basis. How would you get started?

I think the best way is online advertising such as on freelance.com, Facebook, Google, and other sites. You should have your own website to link to from your advertisements. You will know if you can do this business or not.

Be aware of a pitfall in this kind of work. Some people will not like what you write for them while others may love your work. Don't let negative comments discourage you, if you know you are a good writer. Just find another contract to do, or find a new writer to work for.

I will not go into any more detail on this business, but be sure to read the general business requirements in the Appendix.

40. Become a Tutor

If you are or have been a teacher, a professor, an engineer, or a professional in some field where you are good at mathematics, chemistry, physics, a language, or any discipline that students many times need help with, you could become a tutor. This could be a good part-time income for a working person, or supplementary income for a retired person.

Another possibility is to start a tutoring business where you have several associates that assist you and tutor students in various areas, allowing your business to take care of a number of students at they same time.

Note, that if you recruit associates, they should either be partners in the business, or contractors if they are on a temporary work basis.

Whether you work as an individual, or as a multi-person business, remember that you must always treat your students with the utmost respect and kindness, no matter how slow the student is, or what his behavior is. Be prepared for the students who do not want to be tutored and are only there because parents have forced them to go.

These students will act hostile to you and will be resistant to your teaching. If the behavior is unmanageable, you have two options: 1) try to struggle through with the student, or 2) advise the parents that their child is not cooperating and that he or she is wasting your time. In the second case you might ask the parents not to bring the student to you again (unless he or she changes their attitude.)

Refund their money and go on with someone else. But remember that your business will depend on word of mouth advertising so you want to do the best tutoring job you can do with all your students. You will do better if you can tutor on higher levels restricting your work to college students.

College students will only come to you if they are serious about learning (but you could still have to put up with a lot of complaints, for example, "I just can't do it." or "I still don't understand it." Be patient. Some students have to hear the same thing over several times before it sinks in.

To get started, tell all your friends and acquaintances that you will be tutoring, and to spread the word about what you do. You should also place a small advertisement in your local newspaper and perhaps set up a website describing what subjects you tutor in, what hours you work, and how to make an appointment with you.

You can work out of your home, or in some public place such as a local library. Some libraries have rooms that you can arrange to use at a certain time.

When you are tutoring, it is always a good idea to have someone else around when you are working to protect yourself from false allegations from students, especially when working with children or under-age individuals.

I will not go into more detail on this business but be sure to read about the general business requirements in the Appendix.

41. Become a Contract English Teacher

If you are an American or an Englishman, and you have some teaching experience, you may be interested in teaching English in a foreign country. For example, there is a constant demand for English teachers in China. Of course you have to be willing to travel and handle all of the details of living in a foreign land.

One thing that will help you in the foreign country is to also know the language of that country. So before you decide to go to the foreign country you should either already know the foreign language or you should learn it before you go. Make sure you have all the proper documents with you when you enter a foreign country, your passport, your visa permit, your regular ID papers, and any special documents you will need.

Make sure you know exactly what documents you need before you leave. Talk with knowledgeable people about the country you are going to and find out what kinds of problems you could encounter on your visit. Guard your passport with your life. Note that when you stay at a hotel in a foreign country, the hotel will ask you to give them your passport until you leave (and pay your bill.) That is normal and should not be a problem for you as long as you follow the rules.

Check with your country's embassy before you leave, and also got to your embassy for help, if you run into any serious problems when you get there. I will not go into any more detail on this work. Be sure to check the general business requirements in the Appendix. In addition, research what your country's tax laws are concerning your earnings in a foreign land. One more piece of advice. Never carry large amounts of cash on you. Instead use traveler's checks, and credit cards, but not debit cards.

When you get paid, wire all funds, you don't intend to spend in the foreign land, to your bank account in your home country. You can't leave or enter a country with a large amount of cash on you or in your luggage. If you did you would almost certainly arouse suspicion and be in serious trouble.

42. Beauty Counselor (for the ladies)

If you know a lot about make-up and how to apply it to good effect, you could make a good beauty counselor. You might also be able to use your knowledge as an Avon or Mary Kay representative.
So how would get your business started? First of all contact all of your lady friends and acquaintances, and tell them what you plan to do. You may offer your contacts a bounty for any people they refer to you that use your services. You should also place a small advertisement in your local newspaper.
Do not spend a lot of money on advertising until you know how well your business is received by the public. This business is one of those that are hard to start and keep going. But if you have a friendly personality, determination, and you are highly skilled in your work, word will spread that you do a good job.
Keep your charges fair and reasonable and try to be competitive with the beauty shops. Don't get into hair cutting or other activities that you will

have to meet state and local requirements that usually include a long time of study in a cosmetology school to get your certificate (unless that's what you want to do, more power to you dear.)

Along with your beauty counseling you can sell your favorite beauty products that you use to your customers. You could do this work in your home to start with, but eventually you may want to rent some space in a high traffic area such as a mall or shopping center. I will not go into any more detail on this business. Be sure to read the general business requirements in the Appendix.

43. Musician, Performing Arts

Do you have a performing talent, such as in music, playing an instrument or singing, dancing, acting, or maybe a combination of talents? Do you want to use your talent as your profession? If you do not, skip this section. But a lot of people have a great talent and don't know that they do, or they are afraid to step out and try to exercise their talent professionally.

Let us imagine that you do have a talent. First you must practice, practice, and practice, until you are expert in your art. An audience will not tolerate even the smallest mistake, like a missed note, a wrong note, going flat, forgetting your lines, or whatever the mistake might be, you will be considered an amateur or worse a "flop". The 'no mistakes' performance is the difference between an amateur and a professional in the performing arts.

You might have your own style, your own interpretation, and a unique voice or spin on your work, but you can't make any mistakes. For example, let's say that you want to play piano at an up-scale bar or club. First you will have to have your musician's union card. That is the first requirement in the professional's credentials. You will have to have someone to sponsor you: that you are eligible to be allowed into the union as a professional musician. Even after you get your union card, you will still have a long road ahead of you. You will have to get gigs in the not-so up-scale places or 'joints' before you will be able to move up the scale in prestige and pay. You will move up only if you are really a good performer and you impress people with your performances. But keep in mind that there are a lot of good, if not great performers, that never get the recognition they deserve. It is sometimes being at the right place at the right time, and meeting the right people who can help you to get better engagements. So what else could you do with your talent that would provide immediate cash in your pocket?

Consider being a teacher, a tutor, or even opening a school, such as a dancing school (these are popular and do a lot of business if you are a good teacher.) There are also acting schools, and of course music schools. The latter are harder to get going. If you decide to open a school, you will need a brick and mortar building or a rent a store front or loft somewhere.

You will have overhead costs of the building or the rental space. But if you do have a good talent and you want to take advantage of it in a professional manner, don't be afraid to step out and try. At least you know that you did try and gave it your best.

I will not go into more detail on this area of work, profession, or business, but if you are planning to do business in the performing arts, be sure to read the general business requirements in the Appendix.

44. Yard Decorations

The yard decoration business is a low capital investment business. You will have to buy some decorations such as black balloons (for your 40th birthday occasions), and various kinds of signs, and figurines. Other than the decorations you will probably need some kind of a covered truck such as a small panel truck.

You can operate the business out of your home as long as you don't put up signs on your property hawking your business, or have customers coming and going from your home. Your advertisements may be in the Yellow Pages, on a website, and maybe a few small newspaper ads. To get your business going, tell all your friends and acquaintances that you are starting a yard decorating business for special occasions, and maybe do one free decoration for your friends to show what you can do.

Another incentive you can provide to your friends and customers is a money bounty of some amount for referrals that result in a sale. Use your imagination to find cute decorations for various occasions, such as birthdays, new babies, and other occasions. An extension of this business is Christmas decorating, but this is a more complex and difficult undertaking.

Be sure to read the general business requirements in the Appendix.

45. Make Boutique Soap

Making soap can be done at home or in your garage. I recommend the "cold process" as the easiest way to make soap. I also recommend making it yourself from scratch so that you have complete control over the formula, process, and the ingredients, as opposed to using the melt and mold process which is easier but not very creative.

The so-called cold process is not entirely cold as the lye (sodium hydroxide), when mixed into water, will react chemically to reach a temperature of approximately 200 degrees Fahrenheit. There are a lot of recipes available online that you can find on Google by doing a search on "how to make soap".

Basically the cold process involves first making your lye solution consisting of one part lye and 3 parts of distilled water. The process is hazardous. Always wear rubber gloves and goggles from start to finish. Always pour lye into water, not water into lye, as the latter will result in a dangerous reaction causing possible harm to you. The second step is to mix your oils, melted fats, essential oils, nutrients, and any fragrance you want into the oil mix. (This is called the 'acid' mix because the lye and water mix is the caustic ingredient.) Mixing the fats and oils is the creative portion of the process where you can put in the kind of oils and fats you choose to make your soap unique.

You can use all vegetable base fats and oils or animal fats if you want to. Most people will want soap that is organic and vegetarian based, and not animal fat based. Note that animal fats are cheaper to use and you could still call your soap 'organic' if the bulk of the oil you use is animal based (for example, using lard.) The final step is to mix the lye solution with the melted oils at the same temperature.

After it has been mixed and reaches the correct state (see link below), it is poured into molds, insulated for slow cooling, removed when set-up, and allowed to 'cure' for several weeks. Always follow a recipe carefully, take safety precautions, and make sure your containers and mixing equipment will withstand the 200 degrees Fahrenheit. Read about the complete process at the link below before you start.

It is up to you what kind of soap you want to make. But remember that your most likely ultimate customers are women, so you should make your soap according to market demand. Other than making the soap itself, the major problems with this business are first, arranging for distribution in stores or online.

Second you must have decorative and attractive packaging to make sales. Fragrance is also very important. Of course, price, size and shape of the soap bars are also important. Otherwise, this is a business that you can be creative with and offer unique products with desirable characteristics for your customers.

Make sure that your soap is not like the soaps sold in Wal-Mart or other mass-market stores. There is a good website that is a good place to get started with instructions, recipes, materials, and molds that it sells. Here is the website link:

http://www.soap-making-resource.com/cold-process-soap-making.html

Be sure to read the general business requirements in the Appendix.

46. Make Specialty Candles

Making candles is another business where you can be creative. Just don't make any candles that can be bought at Wal-Mart. You can choose the kind of wax you want to use, paraffin (from petroleum) based, or vegetable based (soy wax.) You can add dye to get the color you want, and fragrance to make it appealing to customers. Personally, I don't like the smell of ordinary paraffin wax candles.

To make a business out of making candles, your candles must look good, smell good, and be reasonably priced. Packaging must be attractive to customers. The best distribution will be through boutiques or online. You will have to work hard to establish your market and distribution. You will probably have to send samples to prospective distributors or boutique shops to get approved and receive orders for your candles.

You should have a good website to sell candles directly and to show your distributors that you are a serious business. Anybody can make candles, but remember that your marketing will be to women and you must appeal to women's tastes.

I will not go into more details on this business but there is a very good website that has the information and materials you need to get started:

http://www.lonestarcandlesupply.com/?gclid=CI 3M9Zbs-68CFQOFnQodcy91SQ

Be sure to read the general business requirements in the Appendix.

47. Make Jewelry

If you are good with your hands and working on small things, you might be able to make custom jewelry for customers. For example, let's say that you want to specialize in diamond engagement rings. People are always getting engaged and good quality diamond engagement rings at low prices are always in demand.

Yes, it will take some investment in jeweler's equipment, some loose diamonds, and a variety of settings. The average 1.0 carat round white diamond in a gold setting will sell retail for about $1000 at a typical jewelry store.

Did you know you can buy natural white cut 1 carat diamonds for as low as $250? I will show a link to one source of wholesale diamonds here. But carefully check out any source you plan to buy diamonds from. I don't necessarily recommend this site. I list it as an example:

http://www.ecrater.com/p/10577590/certified100-ct-natural-white-diamonds

Here is a source of ring settings of various kinds and materials:

http://www.firemountaingems.com/Shop/Ring-Settings?/

I don't guarantee the above company either. You must verify your own sources of materials.

So how would you handle the production and marketing of diamond engagement rings (for example?) One way would be to have a website set up where you show a few pictures of your work and other information about your products. You can allow your customer to select from settings and diamonds that you can obtain from your verified sources, but do not make the rings in advance.

You could have a very small stock of settings and a few diamonds ready to install, but you really only need to order the setting and the diamond after the customer has placed his order and you have the money. Then you order the setting and the diamond, if you do not already have stock ready to assemble and ship.

You must give the customer confidence in your business. Offer a money-back guarantee within a reasonable period of time, say ten days, if the customer is not satisfied. The following site (Blue Nile) is an example of a successful online jewelry business. It also has good information on diamonds:

http://www.bluenile.com/

Also get listed with The Better Business Bureau and whatever other sites you can obtain listing with. Below are some organizations that you may be able to get certified and listed with.

You will have to do some research to find out how to get listed and what kind of certification you can obtain from each organization (and how much will it cost you.) You may have to take a short course in jewelry techniques, and pass a test, to get certified, but you do not need a college degree:

http://www.jewelers.org/

http://www.americangemsociety.org/

http://www.mjsa.org/

Also tell your friends and acquaintances that you are designing and making quality engagement rings. Carry a few samples with you for show and tell. Seeing, is believing. You may place a few small newspaper advertisements occasionally in your local area. You may be able to find a jeweler who will assemble the diamonds and settings you provide for you, but more than likely, any jeweler you contact prefers to sell his own products and does not want you competing against him with lower prices.
So you should learn how to install the diamonds in the settings yourself. You will need some small tools and a jeweler's torch to heat up the prongs of the setting so they can be safely set to hold the diamond firmly.
You may also get some requests to repair broken settings, so you should know how to silver solder settings for repairs. This will not be an easy business to do and get started, but there is a good

income to be made, if you are successful. For a simple example, suppose you can assemble, process, and ship, 25 engagement rings per day at an average price of $1000. This will be $25,000 in revenue each day.

If your gross profit averages $500 per ring, your gross income for the day is $12,500. That is not a bad day's work! You may need someone to handle telephone sales, online marketing, order processing, and someone to handle shipping. Try to use only contract workers instead of employees.

As your skill and business becomes stronger, you may be able to expand your marketing reach by affiliating with Amazon.com and setting up an Ebay online store. I will not go into any more details on this business. You will know whether this business is for you or not.

Be sure to read the general business requirements in the Appendix.

48. Sell Hot Dogs

If you have limited funds and enjoy working with food, you may want to do a simple business that you can operate part-time or full-time. What would you need to have a successful hot dog business?

The simplest way would be to by a hot dog cart that is made of stainless steel for the purpose. If you are handy with metal working, you could possibly make your own cart from plans. Here is a link to the "Malibu" hot dog cart I show as an example of a manufactured cart (I don't necessarily recommend this company or site, or guarantee the quality of this cart.)

http://www.dreammakerhotdogcarts.com/hot-dog-carts/malibu/malibu-features.php

Here is another site with some drawings of a cart:

http://peterthorpe.me/hotdogcartstore/dev/titan_schematics.php

There are a lot of used carts for sale which you can find by searching on Google.
Another way is to have a food truck that you can easily drive to places where you can do a good business. (See business no. 53 for a description of the food truck business.)
I have occasionally seen food trucks for sale on "sell-your-own" car and truck lots. You can also search on Google or Ebay to find used food trucks. A third way is to buy a trailer home or motor home and convert it into a hot dog stand or food van. In the south we see a number of these conversions from trailers and buses.
Sometimes the converted buses even use some of the seats inside where a customer can sit down and eat. The converted trailers and buses usually sell Mexican foods, but you could sell hot dogs and sandwiches if you are not in a Southern area. With a trailer, bus, or motor home conversion,

you will need to make arrangements to park it in a lot close to a good source of business, such as a manufacturing plant, a shopping center, or an office center.

Another way is to rent a piece of land somewhere in a good business location, and build a wooden hot dog stand in the more traditional manner (if local zoning regulations allow it.) Finally, you might rent a store front where you set up your hot dog business.

But let's go back to a simple hot dog cart that you might set up on a street corner in a high traffic area.

If you are working by yourself, there are some difficulties that you will face. How to you get your cart to your business location if you live some distance away? Most people haul their hot dog cart with a pick-up truck, but you will need a place to park your truck close to your business location, unless you leave your cart hooked to your truck trailer hitch (Your hot dog cart must have good wheels, an axle, and a trailer hitch tang if you are going to haul it with your truck.)

How do you handle money and make hot dogs at the same time in a sanitary manner? As far as keeping your hot dogs hot and the buns soft, you must have a good cart that will keep your hot dogs in hot water or on a grill and your buns steamed but not too soft. Carts usually have propane gas heaters for the grill and a hot water tank.

To be sanitary in your food handling, use only tongs to pick up the hot dogs, and pick up the buns with a piece of waxed paper or food handling paper (do not touch any food you serve with your bare hands after you have handled money.

Also if you wear gloves, contaminated gloves are just as bad as dirty hands.) Most customers will want condiments such as ketchup, mustard, and sweet relish. Some customers like "Slaw Dogs", or "Sauer Kraut Dogs".

Keep control of your condiments and your other food options, to control costs. Don't let customers handle your condiments or serving tools, for sanitary reasons. Use plastic squeeze bottle dispensers for mustard and ketchup, and keep a cover over the relish and the other cold food toppings you might have.

A good hot dog cart will have small tanks and covers for condiments. The condiment tanks should be kept cold, especially in hot weather. Don't leave a wipe rag loose on the top of your stand. Keep it out of view.

Follow the above sanitation rules regardless of whether you have a cart, a food truck, a bus, a trailer, a shack, or a storefront for your business. Remember, in most localities you will have random Health Department inspections.

I will not go into a lot of more details on this business, but be sure to read the general business requirements in the Appendix.

49. Start a Pawn Shop

A pawn shop is inherently a brick and mortar business, but it does not have to be a fancy building. It could be a shack, a store front, an old industrial building, or any building that is reasonable to rent, or better yet, buy the property if you like it and have the capital. But it should be a good location that people will notice when they drive buy.

It does not have to be in a fancy neighborhood. In fact it is probably better to set up in a lower economic level neighborhood where people are more likely to come to you store to sell something, or pawn something they own.

Buyers will find you wherever you are located if they are serious about finding a bargain priced item of some kind. How does the business work? It's basically buying or pawning items at a low cost and re-selling at a good price.

The profit on any given item should be at least 20% or better. You need to cover your overhead costs and have enough net profit each year to provide yourself a good income. What kind of stock should you buy and sell?

You should stick to items that you know well what they are worth and that you know that there is a market for the item. For example, maybe you know tools of all kinds. Tools are a popular item with men, especially men who are mechanics or who work in the trades. There are also possible extensions to this business.

You might want to expand into the automobile title business, where you give money on clear titles for cars, and then repossess the vehicle if the customer does not pay his loan back. Admittedly, the title business can be nasty if you have to repossess a customer's vehicle (and sometimes you will not be able to find the vehicle to repossess it.) Another extension of the pawn business is paycheck cashing for a fee (8-10%.)

Finally, once you have built up a good stock of items, you may wish to advertise some of your items for sale online, on your own website, Ebay, or Amazon. The latter is a good place to set up an affiliate store selling books, CDs, and DVDs, and a lot of other items. Ebay is a good place to sell tools and equipment of various kinds. There is a lot of potential in the pawn business. You are limited only by your hard work, working capital, and your imagination.

I will not go into more details on this business. Be sure to read the general business requirements in the Appendix.

50. Start a Rental Store

A rental store is a brick and mortar operation. There are franchises for rental businesses. But the franchises are going to be expensive with a high up-front cost to you. It would be difficult to start a rental store for electronics, furniture, and appliances without buying a franchise. But a very popular rental operation that you could start yourself would be one that specializes in tools and equipment.

For example, there is equipment that people don't normally buy but would rent for a day or two, such as augers, back hoes, small bull dozers, trucks, vans, air hammers, compressors, pressure cleaners, and a lot of other light and heavy tools. The main problem with the business is that you will have a lot of money invested in equipment and you will either have to rent or buy a building for your location. There is a factor that helps however.

The equipment you buy has a value that a bank might loan money on as your collateral. You will either have to have the money to start with or you will have to find someone who will loan you money to buy the equipment. Another way that you might be able to finance the business is to form a partnership.

You would be the master partner and normally invest some of your own money in the partnership. Then you would find other partners who think your business looks like a good investment. Each partner would invest a certain amount of money, as required in your partnership agreement (Partnership agreements should only be written by a lawyer as they are usually quite complicated.)

For example, suppose you invest $10,000 yourself in the partnership, and then you enlist ten other partners who each can buy an equal partner share if they also invest $10,000. You now have $110,000 in capital to invest in your business. As the master partner you make all the decisions for the partnership. Once you have this capital you could purchase the initial equipment that you need to get started. Then since you own the equipment, you may be able to borrow another $50,000 or $60,000 from a bank, using the equipment as collateral. It would not be an easy process, but there is no 'easy' business to get started. The financing scheme I just described has been used in the real estate field by real estate operators to finance developments, shopping centers, and apartment complexes. But I am digressing.

To start the rental equipment business, you will need to do some research to determine what rental equipment is in most demand by people. Stop by Home Depot and note what kinds of equipment the store rents out. Once you know what equipment you need to get started, the next thing you need to do is prepare a good business plan for submission to your investors or banks you are trying to loan money from.

I will not go into more details on this business, but be sure to read the general business requirements in the Appendix.

51. Become a Head Hunter

No, I am not talking about the primitive head shrinkers. I am talking about people that have a business finding executives and other people with specialized experience that is in demand by companies around the world or just in a local area. For example, suppose a large company in Chicago is looking for a professional sales manager. The listed salary range is $100,000 and up.

You, as a professional search representative, have several sales managers' resumes in your file or you know someone who is looking for a sales manager's job. You may or may not know a Human Resources person at the company that has the job, or you have a friend or acquaintance that works at the company.

You might select your best candidate. Then you send a short summary of the experience and qualifications of the applicant. If you are successful and your candidate is hired, the company will pay you a finder's fee. The fee might range from 5% to 10%. Usually a reputable employment search representative, such as yourself, does not charge the successful candidate anything.

Obviously, the more people you know in business, and the more contacts you have, the more likely you are to be successful. You can operate out of your home doing business by telephone and online. One other aspect of the business is that you will have to spend time marketing your business.

You can attract candidates for jobs with small advertisements in newspapers and online. But to get known by businesses where you don't know anyone, may require traveling to various businesses, and making appointments with the Human Resources managers. With some money coming in from the business, you may be able to place ads in the slick magazines that business people might read and in national newspapers such as the *Wall Street Journal*, and *USA Today*. The advantage of the business is that it is a low investment start-up. But you will have to work hard to develop customers and employment candidates. I will not go into further details on this business, but be sure to read the general business requirements in the Appendix.

52. Catering

If you are a chef or a good cook, you have expert knowledge of foods and how to prepare them for a sophisticated clientele, you may want to do professional catering. Why would you do this instead of just owning your own restaurant? The main reason is that you don't have to make a large investment in a brick and mortar restaurant, or have to lease space that will be a significant expense each month.
If you install the necessary equipment, you could work out of your own home (if it is allowed by local laws.) Of course you will need the space to cook and prepare your food. Depending on the local regulations, you will most likely have to pass a health inspection also. You must do the

necessary research on your local laws and regulations before you dive into this business. As a part of the business, you would normally need to be able to supply tables, chairs, table clothes, silverware, plates, glass wear, coffee makers, tea pots, and so forth for events such as large dinners in a rented hall.

Some places you cater may have tables and chairs but probably nothing else that you would want to use. So what kinds of events might you cater? There a lot of different possibilities such as wedding parties, anniversaries, club meetings, celebrations, and also in homes that are having some kind of a dinner party or whatever.

If you are a knowledgeable chef or cook you will probably know how to prepare for each event, but always find out from the host what he or she wants you to serve. It could be anything from a seven course meal to cheese on crackers. Some things you need to know about each job: Is there an open bar? Who is going to provide and pay for the liquor and drinks? What tables, chairs, and table service will be available if any?

Before you start, make a list of all the things you will need to know, so you will come to the event with everything you need to do the job in an excellent manner. Also you will usually need plenty of advance scheduling so that you can order any special foods or materials that you will need for each event.

Maintain an accurate scheduling book so you don't get caught in a conflict between different events. For large events, you may have to collect partial payment in advance, especially if you will have a lot of expenses buying special foods and materials. If someone cancels their event, make them pay a healthy penalty cost of say 75% of the full cost.

If they have already paid 50% down for the event, bill them anther 25%. After all, if they cancel, you have lost time that you could have used to make money elsewhere.

How would you get started doing business? You will have to do a little marketing work. Tell all your friends and acquaintances that you are starting a catering business in your area, and tell them you will give them a discount rate on any catering they may want you to do, to introduce your service.

You might also offer a bounty to people that refer customers to you that you cater to. Don't forget to place small advertisements in your local newspaper and high-end magazines. You should also maintain a website with photos of some of the events and the dishes you have catered. But don't spend a lot of money advertising until you know how well your business is doing and whether or not the expense is justified.

I will not go into any more details on this business, but be sure to read the general business requirements in the Appendix.

53. Food Truck

A food truck is similar to the hot dog cart, except that you would probably have hot coffee, snacks, and cold foods such as sandwiches, serving mostly people who want something quick to eat for lunch. If you are really ambitious, you might have a large food truck and also serve breakfast items, such as sausage-egg biscuits, oatmeal, a scrambled egg and sausage plate, or other meals depending on what your customers ask for.

You will have to set your menu according to what people want on your route of customers. If you are going to do a breakfast route, you will have to get up very early in the morning to prepare your food and cover your route. The best routes are in industrial sections where workers start work early and maybe did not have time to fix breakfast at home, or where fast food places are not fast enough. Speed is one of the advantages of your business.

You have your items ready to hand out, usually already packaged in containers of some kind to make your service not only fast but almost instant service. The secret to success is a good route, great clean food, punctuality, and fast easy service. You need to work out your route so you serve the workers before they have to start work. Each industrial plant or office building will have a certain morning shift start time (but not always different from each other.)

You can't be at two places at the same time, unless you have more than one truck and service man, so you will just have to learn which locations are the best to go to at your serving times. You will need a truck, either designed to be a food truck, or you will have to modify an existing van or box truck for the work. So you will need some money to get this business started. You can find food trucks for sale on the Internet. Here is just one link as an example:

http://roadstoves.com/food-trucks-for-sale.html

I will not go into more details on this business, but be sure to read the general business requirements in the Appendix.

54. Barbecue Cart

In the barbecue business you will need some basic equipment and some barbecue cooking skill. Most people like the charcoal pit barbecue method because of its superior taste. I present here a website that sells the kind of equipment that would be suitable. But I don't necessarily recommend this company. (You should do your own research.)

http://www.belson.com/grills.htm?gclid=CNrx9L T0m7ACFYmR7QodbmlcYQ&WT.mc_id=510 &WT.srch=1

In the type of business I am suggesting here you would make arrangements to park your cart in a good location that has a lot of traffic, but is not expensive. I have seen barbecue carts in gas station lots, in shopping center parking lots, and sometimes in front of stores such as Kroger and Wal-Mart.

Some vendors have rented locations where they work on every week-end. Other vendors have arranged with a grocery owner to barbecue and sell the grocery store's meat. One example I saw at a Kroger store was a vendor selling a rack of barbecued baby back ribs for $9.99.

It was a one-day affair arranged with the Kroger store and Kroger allowed the vendor to put a small sign on the front of the store advertising the event in advance.

The vendor had a large charcoal-wood pit barbecue cart that he set up right next to the store's front door.

Some vendors will use the single day event and others prefer to have a regular location. At the Kroger event, the vendor did not have to pay rent for the location, but he no doubt had to pay Kroger for the meat he barbecued.

So there are ways to operate this business without a large overhead cost. It is up to you how you want to operate this business, and you will know if it is a business you can handle yourself.

You will have to work hard, starting early in the morning and working all day to sell your product. I will not go into more detail on this business, but be sure to read the general business requirement in the Appendix. Also research your local health department requirements and regulations on the outdoor food vendor.

55. Start a Lingerie Online Store

For you ladies (and men too) you can buy lingerie of various kinds wholesale and re-sell it retail on your own website. One good item is pantyhose which are available at true wholesale prices from various vendors. I don't recommend any particular vendor but I list some links here as examples of vendors you might check out to start your research.
Of course you will have to contact various vendors for various items you wish to handle, and work out the details of how you will do business with each one.

http://www.dollardays.com/i327560-wholesale-sensations-sheer-pantyhose.html?utm_source=google&utm_medium=cpc&gclid=CMKx1sfSnLACFQcEnQodA048Xw

http://www.wmsclothing.com/cgi-bin/category/BraSets

http://www.lingerie4wholesale.com/Wholesale_Hosiery_s/28.htm

To get your business going, first tell all your female friends (and men looking for gifts for their wives and girlfriends) that you are starting a lingerie website with bargain pricing. When you first start, concentrate on low price high popularity items that appeal to a large cross section of women.

Don't be greedy with a high mark-up over your wholesale prices so you can compete and get volume sales started quickly. Your main problem will be getting a good website set up that will allow you to process credit cards of various kinds, Pay Pal, and other typical payment methods. Your site needs to be attractive and with fast loading of the home page and product pages.

As a help to get started, you might place inexpensive advertisements on Facebook and Google. Try to get your business affiliated with major retailing operations like Amazon.com, Ebay, and others to increase your web presence. You can also do a blog that highlights some of your products and other useful information for women.

Make use of Twitter where you can post short product announcements, or just a general 'tweet' on your business. Twitter is friendly to businesses of all kinds that tweet their messages every day. I use Facebook, Google, and Twitter to promote my various e-books that I have published.

Facebook has the advantage of allowing you to get many subscribers and friends, as well as joining groups that may have thousands of users where you can also post your messages. You have to be careful about promoting your business on Facebook and Google as there are certain restrictions and you don't want to be too blatant in your posts. Of course there no is trouble placing paid-for advertisements.

Here is a site that helps you set up a complete online business website including credit card processing and other services (but check the cost, and do your own research.)

http://www.volusion.com/

Using a commercial website that helps you create a site may be ok to get started with, but if you want a really fast website that does not have a large software overhead, you should get a professional programmer to create your website. I will not go into any more detail on this business, but be sure to read the general business requirements in the Appendix.

56. Start a Vegetable Stand

Here is a very basic business that a lot of people can do even if you are not a farmer. If you are a farmer you simply find a location set up some tables and put out your vegetables for sale on nice days. Your tables do not have to be fancy. They should light weight so you can hall them to any location with your pick-up truck. A pick-up truck is almost a necessity for this business.

If you have a permanent location you may be able to put a permanent stand for your business. It is good to have some shade over your work position but not over the produce because your vegetables will look better in direct sunlight. Of course if you have some vegetables that are sensitive to heat and sunlight, you should also have some shade for those items.

If you are not a farmer, you do the same thing, but first you go to the farmers market in your area (most towns have at least one), and get there as soon as they open. Farmers markets usually open about 5AM, so if you want to buy the best produce, get there when they open up. Buy items that are common and sell well, such as green beans, carrots, cabbage, potatoes, onions, and watermelons when in season. Don't buy vegetables that will not sell well in your area. Of course if you live in China, you would buy Chinese vegetables. Don't accept the farmers posted price. Haggle with him for a better price. You should have bargaining power because you are probably going to buy in large quantities that you can put out on your stand or tables for as long as three days, depending on how well each item will keep without refrigeration outdoors. When you pack up what remains from sales during the day, you could put the items on ice in your garage or shed. That will help keep them fresh. Never freeze vegetables. You need to set up in a high traffic location that does not cost you a lot of rent money for the space. I have seen good locations in front of high traffic gasoline stations, or where other vendors have stands set up. Don't be afraid of competition.

More people will stop and look if there are several stands set up in the location. Make sure you are not violating local zoning regulations where you set up. Usually areas that are zoned for retail business are ok, but sometimes not. So you must do your research first. You need a street vendor's license almost everywhere.

You don't want to be kicked off your spot by the police. They might even give you a very expensive ticket. You will know ahead of time if you can do this business or not.

I will not go into more detail on this business but be sure to read the general business requirements in the Appendix.

57. House Painting

Do you like to be your own boss and work outdoors? You don't mind a little hard work that is sometimes a little messy? Heights don't bother you, and you don't mind climbing a ladder to the third floor level of a house? House painting is not a real easy business but the average job will pay you $1000 or more for about three days of work. If you can get two jobs each week steadily (when the weather is good), you could average $6000 to $8000 a month in a painting season. That is not bad pay for a little hard work. If you work in Florida or California, or other areas where weather is good for painting year round, you will do well. But how many years can you do that kind of physical work before you have to stop because of age or health?

One answer is that you expand your business by contracting workers to paint for you on jobs that you arrange. At that point you are a manager of your business, locating jobs, and supervising the painters you have contracted, without actually doing much physical work yourself. So what do you need to get started?

At the minimum you will need a truck or van rigged to carry two or three ladders and maybe some scaffolding. You should also have some mechanical means for mixing your paint, especially the 5 gallon pails. You will have to do some advertising and marketing work. Get bonded, licensed, and insured. A good place to advertise is in the *Yellow Pages*.

Also tell all of your friends and acquaintances that you are going into the painting business and you are offering bounties for any jobs that someone refers to you and that result in a job. Get business cards printed with your name, business name, and telephone number. Tack up your cards on the bulletin boards in *Lowes* and *Home Depot* for contractors.

Also visit various paint supply stores and leave your cards at these stores. Most paint stores have painting contractor business cards on their counters. In the process of visiting paint stores, try to find a good paint store that carries good quality paint and has good pricing for quantity purchases, for example paint in 5 gallon pails. The better the quality of the paint you use, the better the guarantee you can give the customer. For example, if you use 15 year paint and you do a proper painting job, you could safely give the customer a 5 year warranty on your work. Your warranty should not be a money-back guarantee, but a guarantee of repair of any defects in your work. Before you quote a job to a potential customer, you should estimate the approximate square feet of the house exterior so you will know how much paint you will need, and you can be sure to include that into your estimate for your cost of painting the house. Then you can give your customer an accurate quotation that is competitive so you have a good chance of getting the job. So what is a proper painting job? If you are interested in this business, you probably already know how to paint a house. The important points are first, the wood must be dry, the temperature must be in the correct range for the kind of paint you are using, and the surface must be prepared by scraping, sanding, or burning off any loose paint. Any cracks or spaces should be calked, rough spots sanded down, and an application of a suitable primer coat is applied when necessary (on bare spots.) It is better to apply two thin coats that one heavy coat. Then your work will look better and be more durable. Something to be careful about is inside painting jobs. Inside jobs are difficult. Even when a house is vacant it is difficult, and a lot more difficult if you have to cover and move around furniture.

So if you are going to do an inside job, make sure your quote it high enough to be worth your time. It is good work though, in cold or bad weather, when you can't paint outside. An extension of your painting business is an option available to good house painters that have saved some capital. Basically the way this optional business works, is to buy houses that are generally in good shape but need some freshening up with new paint. You paint the house inside and out to make the house look newly renovated and repaired (you could do some minor repairs as needed, but don't do major renovations.) Then you sell the house for a higher price than you paid, to pay for your time and materials, plus some profit over your original cost.

Two young men in the Haight-Ahsbury district in San Francisco became millionaires doing what I just described. They started painting houses with fresh bright colors and then sold them for a nice profit. It caught on with others who started painting their houses, and it resulted in re-vitalization of the area.

I will not go into more detail on this business, but be sure to read the general business requirements in the Appendix.

58. Small Repairs on Houses

When I was fifteen years old I did small repairs on houses part-time after school and week-ends. Usually it was for older folks who needed a little help. I was usually able to take care of simple little repairs and occasionally moving an appliance or some furniture. There were a lot of things I did not do because they were too difficult for me, or too big a job.

But there were also a lot of things even a fifteen year old boy could do. I tell the story just to point out that there are a lot of people who can't do, or don't want to do, even little repair jobs, or tasks around their home. Another fact is that most contractors do not want to do small jobs because they are too busy making big money on big jobs (and I don't blame them at all.)

So if you need a little extra money, or need some employment, which is sometimes hard to find, you might try to get some small repair jobs to do. You could place a small advertisement in your local newspaper, get some business cards printed, and distribute some flyers around your local area describing what you do. If you do a good job, you may get repeat business.

Now there is also a potential for advancement in the repair business. Suppose you gradually learn to do larger and larger jobs. You might take a short course in heating, ventilating, and air conditioning (HVAC.) If you do progress to larger and larger jobs, eventually you may become a general contractor.

But even if you never become a general contractor, I think you can make a living on small repair jobs, or at least a part-time income.
 Be sure to read the general business requirements in the Appendix.

59.0 Wood Floor Restoration

This is a business that no one wants to do. At least I have not found anyone that will do it at a reasonable price. It is a lot of work. A typical old wooden floor will be well worn with deep scratches and usually the finish is totally worn off in places. There could also be water damage, rot, and termite damage.
So this work is not easy. You may have to replace sections of wood which will not be easy to do. You will have to find wood that matches as close as possible, and if the boards are interlocking you have to figure out how to replace damaged spots without have to tear out large sections of the floor.
Generally, you will have to sand the entire floor and then refinish it. If the house is empty it will be a little easier. But if you have to work around furniture and move it around, it will take a lot more time and physical work. Sometimes a floor is so bad it will be cheaper to replace the entire floor. If this is the case, you should be ready to tear out the whole floor and replace it with the correct wood to meet the customer's desires.

You will have to have connections with flooring material vendors such as *Home Depot, Lowes*, and others in your area to get the best materials and prices. Of course your quotations to your customers will include the cost of all materials, your labor, contract labor you might need to use, and of course a proportional mark-up for your profit.

You should have some skilled people lined up that you can draw on in case you need help. Eventually, you can branch out to handle general flooring jobs, such as carpeting, and tiled floors.

So how can you get started?

You should have a panel truck painted with your name, business name, and telephone number.

You will need some basic hand tools, and some power tools such as a floor sander. You can place small advertisements in your local newspaper, and place your business cards on the contractor bulletin boards at local flooring suppliers.

As you progress and build a reputation, you may decide to open a full service brick and mortar store, selling carpeting and other flooring material, and providing installation services, as well as continuing your floor restoration business, (if you still want to do that kind of work.)

I will not go into more detail on this business, but be sure to read the general business requirements in the Appendix.

60. Install Solar Auxiliary Power Systems

If you live in a city like I do where the electric power can go off for 4 or 5 days, frequently, you would probably like to have an auxiliary power back-up system for your home. There are a lot of people who would, if they could afford to install it. So here is the business:

You find houses that are candidates for solar power. The candidate house is usually one of the more expensive homes, with a long roof section that faces south, so it will catch the sun almost all day long. Preferably, there are no tall trees around the house that will shade the roof (check out mainly new developments.) Another plus is that the house is on a street that runs east and west and the front of the house faces north. Why? Because most people don't want the solar panels on the front side roof of the house where some people think they look ugly. (Yes, it is dumb to think that they are ugly, but that is human nature. Myself, I would be proud to show that my house is saving energy that would otherwise come from burning coal or gas.)

Anyway if you are doing the marketing for your business, you could knock on the potential customer's, door or leave a flyer with your business name, what you do, and your telephone number on it. You will also have to do other marketing as well as the direct marketing.

Local newspaper ads, local high end magazines, contractor mailing services, posters on busses, and whatever other means you can afford to do.

So how would the solar power system work? There are several different ways, but the way I would set it up is to use the solar panels to charge up batteries.

Once the batteries are charged, they are maintained with a 'trickle charge', and the excess solar power is dumped back into the utility lines. By law the utility has to accept your excess power if it meets standards, and they have to credit your power bill accordingly. If the utility power fails, your power transfer switch will connect your power inverter to your house power lines with the inverter drawing power from your solar charged batteries.

You will need a solar power converter that converts the voltage from the solar panels to the correct voltage to charge your batteries. So how much power can you get from the solar panels? Depending on where you live and how much sunshine you normally have, a typical power output per square foot of solar panel is 8 to 10 watts (when the sun is shinning brightly.)

For example, suppose you have a house with a large section of roof so that you could have a solar panel of 15 feet high by 50 feet long, or 750 square feet times 8 watts per square foot equals 6000 watts of power.

Now if you have say 4 hours of good sunshine per day on the average (no power generation at night of course) then you will generate about 500 kilo-watt hours per month (using an efficiency factor of 70% for your inverter conversion efficiency), or about 42% of the average home power usage of about 1200 kilo-watt hours per month.

So you could save about 42% on your power bill each month. But suppose you used some of the solar power you generate to charge a bank of 100 amp-hours batteries (like ordinary automobile batteries.) If you have 48, 12V batteries in your battery bank, you then have 1200 amp-hours times 12 volts equals 57.6 kilo-watt hours of emergency back-up power.

So now you have about 24 hours of battery back-up of your home's average power usage, just using your batteries as a power source (assuming you have no useful sunlight during the utility power outage.) If you stretch your stored power by shutting down lights and appliances you don't really need, and you get some sunshine to help, you might be able to have enough power for your home for a week or more, depending on how much power you use.

You don't need a smelly and noisy gasoline powered generator. I would like to do this at my house, even if the power savings never paid for the cost, and I think a lot of people feel the same way. So this is the business. Is it risky? Yes, but your capital investment is low. The customer pays for all the labor, materials, and equipment you install at his house.

You will need the help of a qualified electrician to install the automatic power transfer switch connection to the utility lines. If you have some basic electrical and mechanical skills, you can do the rest.

I will not go into more details on this business, but be sure to follow the general business requirements in the Appendix.

61.0 Build Patio Decks

If you like carpentry work and like to be creative, you might consider building patio decks for people. If you do a good job you will get plenty of work. This business has the advantage of little capital investment.

You don't even really need a truck as you can get all of the materials you need to build a deck delivered directly to the customer's house by the company that you buy the wood from. So how would this business work, assuming you have a customer lined up?

The first thing is to find out what the customer wants and how much he or she is willing to spend on their deck. To find out what they want, you might have some stock pictures of various decks to show them. There a lot of books available on patio deck designs that you can use to get ideas from.

Once you have an idea what the customer wants, make a drawing of your design with some basic dimensions. Show it to the customer to make sure that he or she likes your design. Once you have settled on a design, you can make an estimate of the cost of materials, and then quote the customer your price which includes material, labor, any concrete work that needs to be done (you may need a concrete contractor to do the concrete work), and your profit.

Be competitive. Quote the lowest prices you can and still make a reasonable profit. Why? Because, once people find out you are reasonably priced and do a good job, they will tell others and you will get more jobs to do. Another hint: Don't start one job, get partly done with it and then go start another job. Some contractors do this to get as many jobs going at the same time as they can to 'lock up' customers.

But I can tell you that this just makes customers mad and they will not give you any more work and maybe even 'bad mouth' you to others, or write bad notes about you on reputation websites.

But how can you get started in this business? The first thing to do is a lot of study on the subject. What kind of construction should you use? Nails, screws, wooden pegs?

What kinds of woods are best? What kinds of sealants are best? How much load will certain designs support? If 25 people are dancing on your deck will it handle the load or collapse? How can you prevent termite infestation? How should the deck be cleaned? How long will your design(s) take to build? How much lumber will be required? How many feet of planks? How many feet of beams? What should the dimensions of planks and beams be? How much will all the wood cost? How long will your deck design last for your customer?

One thing that would help you is to have some good computer software and a computer you can use to help make professional drawings. Some people can draw good enough to make good looking sketches or drawings that the customer will like. One thing that will impress your customers is to bring along a laptop computer that you have already made a drawing on your computer that you can call up and show the customer on his or her premises.

Before you start building a patio deck for someone, make sure that you get a building permit, and that your design will be in conformance with local building codes. Once you have completed a deck, take a good picture of it and note your price. Make a 'show and tell' scrapbook with your photos and bring it along to show your potential customer what you have already done.

To get started you will need to do a little marketing. Tell all your friends and acquaintances that you are building decks and offer them a bounty if they refer anyone to you that becomes a paying customer. Place small advertisements in your local newspaper. Set up a website with your business information and photos of the work you have done. Get business cards printed and leave some at various home improvement stores such as Lowes and Home Depot.

Put your business name and phone number on your truck or car. Print flyers and leave them at houses in better neighborhoods where customers are more likely to call you. You should not spend a lot of money advertising in this kind of business. Your customers will come mainly from 'word-of-mouth' referrals.

I will not go into more details about this business, but be sure to read the general business requirements in the Appendix.

62. Become a Real Estate Agent

There are pros and cons to being a real estate agent. As an agent, you do not really have your own business. You are working for a broker. However, after you have a certain amount of time being an agent, depending on local laws, you can take the test to become a licensed broker, which then gives you the opportunity to open your own real estate sales office. Let's cover the cons first, and if you can get through the cons, maybe you have 'the right stuff' to become a real estate agent.

1. You will most likely have to pay a large fee to join the Multiple Listing Service (MLS), depending on what the local real estate multiple listing association requires. In my local area the fee is over $1000 depending on the market conditions at the time. Of course you have to pass the state's real estate agent's test to get your real

estate license, before you can join a real estate firm and the MLS.

2. When you first join a firm, you will have a steep learning curve. There is a maze of forms and procedures you will have to learn at the typical real estate firm, and you may have trouble finding someone who is willing to help you learn. One way around this problem is to join a large firm in your area and become a member of a 'team' of agents that work under one senior agent or broker that works at the firm. As a 'newbie', you may be subject to a lot of ribbing and sometimes even harassment, depending on the firm.

3. It may be a long time before you become skilled enough to make a sale, and even after you become skilled, sales may be few and far between, depending on the market for real estate at the time.

As I am writing this, the real estate market has gone through a massive downturn and housing sales are very weak. So as I am writing this book, real estate sales agents are finding few sales. Even when the market is good you may only make a few sales in a year which will not be enough to provide more than supplementary income for you. The number of sales you make will depend on how hard you work, how many people you can reach out to, and how good you are at closing contracts.

4. Unless you know a lot of people, you will have a hard time making sales in real estate. To

counter this problem, you should join as many organizations as you can, for example the Rotary club, the Masons, and others that have groups in your area. You will have to be friendly, make new friends, and participate in club projects. You will be very busy!

5. You will spend a lot of time running people around town and the countryside, and burning up gasoline, with no results most of the time.

6. You will have to work hard to get new listings and be able to work with cantankerous owners who will not readily negotiate with a buyer to help you close a sale.

7. You may have to meet clients, that you have not met, and go to questionable neighborhoods to show run-down properties that are messy and dirty.

8. In real estate transactions there are a lot of 'gotchas' and traps that you can fall into. You have to be very careful in what you say and do, and what you agree to at all times.

9. There will be a lot of disappointments. There will be sales that fail at the last minute due to some minor problem. Sales that appear to be closed but are killed by some legal fault in the contract, or a faulty deed, or some other hidden problem.

Now if you have gotten this far without getting discouraged, I will list the pros for you.

1. If you work hard, you are always friendly and patient, and if you are good at closing sales you can make a living.

2. If you are an experienced and skilled agent, and you keep working hard at it, you can make a lot of money.

3. When you have enough experience, become well-known, and have a good reputation, you can perhaps become a broker and open your own office. That is a path that could lead to wealth for you.

4. You will learn a lot about properties, the value of properties, the effects of property characteristics on their value, pricing properties, legal requirements, neighborhoods, good properties, bad properties, good deals and bad deals, how to write a real estate sales contract, and a lot of other good information.

5. You will find opportunities in real estate that you might want to take advantage of yourself, such as properties that you can 'flip', properties that you can buy and rent out, properties that are bargains and you want to buy for your own real estate portfolio.

6. Meeting people that are influential and wealthy, making new friends, developing loyal clients that always turn to you when they are buying or selling properties.

7. Developing a satisfying profession and being in a position to help people find the home of their dreams, or at least a home that satisfies them and fits their needs.

So that is the story. Do the pros outweigh the cons? I think they do. But it depends on you, how hard you work, and how much you want to be successful.

I will not go into more details on this business (or profession), but be sure to read the general business requirements in the Appendix.

63. Become a Real Estate Appraiser

This business is a great business to get into. Why? It does not require college, but it does require some appraisal education and some trainee experience. It does not require a capital investment. It does not require a brick and mortar office (you can work out of your home.)

Each job you do pays $400 and upwards for only about ½ hours of work or even less time in most cases (when you have your own business set-up.) If you could do only one job a day, you would still make $2000 a week or more depending on how much you charge. What is the main problem? You will have a lot of competition as there are usually a lot of appraisers available in any sizeable community.

But they all charge about the same prices so your main problem will be to market your services. Who would you market your services to? To the banks and mortgage loan companies in your area. Because you have to work as in intern under a certified appraiser for a period of time, you will learn who the customers for your services will be, once you start your own appraisal service.

So what are the requirements to obtain an appraiser's license? The requirements vary from state-to-state, but usually you must have proof of up to 100 hours of instruction in appraisal education, have from 1000 to 3000 hours of internship or training under a certified appraiser (depending on the level of license you want to obtain), and pass the state test that applies. There are usually several different types of licenses available for different levels of work, and each type requires a certain amount of education and intern hours, as well as a test and a license fee. So it is not that easy to get a full license. You will normally have to get your intern or trainee license first by meeting a minimum education requirement and then pass the test for that license.

If you already have a license in a state, the requirements to get a license in another state are abbreviated. An example is getting a license in Nevada, if you already have a license in California. One thing that helps is that you can usually take the test as many times as you need to, to pass the test, within a limited period of time, for example one or two years.

I will not go into more detail on this business, but be sure to find out what the requirements in your state are, and read the general business requirements in the Appendix. You can easily find the requirements for your state on a Google search using the search phrase "requirements for

appraisal license in _____ " and including
the name of your state.

64. Home Assistance

Because of the advances in medical science,
people are living longer and longer. But there are
some problems. Because people are living longer,
there are more seniors who unfortunately need
help with completing simple tasks and basic
needs at home. Another problem is that a lot of
people cannot afford to go to a nursing home
because they do not have the money, or they do
not have nursing home insurance (which is very
hard to obtain if a person has any pre-existing
conditions.)
So, a lot of people who need assistance are just
staying home. If a person needs qualified nursing
care at home, then a qualified nurse is required to
care for that person. However, a lot of seniors, or
even young people, just need a little help and
assistance to live at home. This is where you
come in.
Both male and female persons can be personal
assistants, depending on the needs of the person
needing assistance and what gender they want to
help them. Most will probably want a female
helper, but some will want a male helper. Home
assistance costs are not low either and usually run
at least $200 or $300 a week or more for full day
assistance. Sometimes only help is needed in the

morning hours, and sometimes all day. In any case, $200 a week is not bad pay for the assistant. What do you need to be successful in this business? First you need a pleasant personality and a lot of patience. Secondly you need to be physically strong, especially if you are helping a large person to move around. So if you have a weak back, forget this kind of work.

Finally, you need to be prepared to handle all kinds of situations, such as very personal needs, to nearly constant help given to someone all day long. You may not get any break time on this job, so you better be prepared for the worst case. Before you accept a job, make sure you do an interview with the person or their guardian to find out exactly what assistance will be needed. Also make sure you get to meet the person who will need assistance. If you don't think you can handle a particular case, turn the job down. It is better if the customer finds someone else that can handle the job. So how would you get started? First, tell all your friends and acquaintances that you will be providing personal assistance to people. Also place a small advertisement in your local newspaper. Have personal references ready to provide to the customer.

When you first start out, be competitive. To get your business going faster, charge a little lower rate than the going rate for your area. If you give good service at a reasonable price, you will have plenty of work. There is also a possibility for expanding your business by contracting others to work for you as personal assistants that you would assign out to various jobs.

If you operate that way, you will spend your time lining up work for your contractors instead of doing the assistance work yourself. Of course you have to charge the customer a little more than you pay your contractor in order to make a profit. Be sure to find out what requirements personal assistants have to meet in your state.

It is a great money-making business if you can manage it. Your capital investment is practically zero. Make each contractor provide their own transportation to and from the job.

will not go into more details on this business, but be sure to read the general business requirements in the Appendix.

65. Home Insulation Testing and Remediation

There are many old houses that have inadequate insulation in their walls and ceilings. These homes that have low insulation R- values, will use more power for air conditioning in the summer (if they have air conditioning) and burning a lot of fuel or power in the winter time. With the high cost of electric power and heating oil, utility bills can be very high for such homes. A good insulation remediation job on an old house can pay for itself on lowered utility bills in a short time. But where does the house need insulation improvement and how can it be remediated? This is where you come in.

You can use a little basic heat transfer physics to measure the heat flow through walls and ceilings with a simple measurement technique. Once you have the temperature data and an estimate of the R-value of the wall (or ceiling, floor, window, door, etc.), you can calculate the heat loss yourself using the formula below, or you can use an online calculator, such as the two listed below listed below.

You will need an infrared thermometer for temperature measurements. You can purchase a good infrared thermometer from your local building supply store. Home Depot has a good selection. One that I like is the General Tools Model #IRT206. It has a laser sighting beam and an LCD display. Rated at 5 stars, it costs approximately $50, as I write this. The website for infrared thermometers at Home Depot is:

http://www.homedepot.com/h_d1/N-5yc1vZc35w/h_d2/Navigation?langId=-1&storeId=10051&catalogId=10053

So how do you measure heat flow through walls, windows, doors, and ceilings to determine the heat loss (or heat leaking into the house when it is hot outside and the air conditioning is running?) If you know some basic algebra there is a simple equation to find heat lost.

First though, you need to find out the R-value of the wall, or whatever the component of the house for which the heat loss is to be measured. The following site provides you with the R-values for different materials and shows how to find the value for a composite of materials.

http://coloradoenergy.org/procorner/stuff/r-values.htm

Now, you use the R-value of the materials of the heat barrier to calculate the heat loss. A wall will usually consist of layers of different materials, such as wood, brick, plaster or wall board (sheet rock), and maybe some insulating material, such as fiber glass, or rock wool. You can make an assumption of what materials are in a wall by noting the inside and outside materials, and by the approximate date of the house.
 For example, a very old house is more likely to have rock wool insulation than fiber glass insulation. Once you have computed the R-value from your knowledge of the type of construction materials and the table given by the above source link, and made measurements of the inside and outside temperatures (or defined the temperatures based on the worst case outdoor temperature for the climate of the location, and using 72 degrees F for the inside of the room), then you have all the data you need to calculate the heat loss of the barrier from the equation

$$Q = A \, (T_{outside} - T_{inside}) \, / \, R\text{-value}$$

where Q is the energy per unit time in BTU per hour, A is the total area of the barrier (area of the wall, the total area of all outside walls, or whatever you are trying to measure the heat loss from) in square feet, and Toutside and Tinside are the Fahrenheit temperatures you measure or define.

If you use the table of R-values given above, your answer will be in BTU per hour (energy per unit time.). With experience, you will use the same R- values for similar homes based on the age of the home and the construction techniques used at the time. Your heat loss calculations may not be absolutely correct but you will get relative values for different barriers (walls, windows, doors, etc.) as long as you are consistent.

Your relative values will allow you to determine if the house has adequate insulation or not. When you define the two temperatures, be sure to use the worst case outside temperatures for the climate, and the typical inside temperature that people usually like to set their thermostats at, for example 72 degrees Fahrenheit. It is always good to measure the actual inside and outside temperatures and calculate the heat loss for the actual day that you are visiting the customer's house.

Then you can tell him how much heat he is losing per hour as you talk. This is always impressive, especially if it is a very hot or cold day. So you have two heat loss calculations to give the customer:

The worst case heat loss for the climate where he or she is located, and the 'actual' measured heat loss value for the day you are there. Another thing that will impress your customers is to use your infrared temperature meter to measure the temperature of the wall that the thermostat is mounted on (as your reference value) and then measure the temperature of walls in other rooms (but not at vent locations.)

If the home has poor insulation, or the heating-cooling vents are not properly distributed between rooms, the temperatures will differ by 2 or 3 degrees or more. If the house needs a better ventilation system, this is your chance to offer to re-design the ventilation ducting system (for a price.).) One more test you can do is to turn off the heating-cooling system for 15 or 20 minutes. Wait a few minutes and then measure the temperatures of each room. Then close all the interior doors to each room and wait about 20 minutes. While waiting you can go outside and measure the temperatures of the exterior walls. After collecting that data go back inside and measure the temperatures of the exterior walls in each room with their doors still closed (Ask the customer to go with you when you go into a room and close the door so you have a witness to what you are doing in that room.) Now compare the new temperatures of each room with the reference temperatures that you started with at the start of the experiment.

If a particular room has changed more than other rooms, then that is a good indication that the room has poor insulation in the walls, ceiling, or floor. How much the average temperatures of the room change during the time period with the heating-cooling system turned off. If little change happens during the 20 minute period, the house insulation is pretty good. In a perfectly insulated home, the temperatures would all be identical (and the R-value would be infinitely high, so no heat loss can be calculated other than zero BTU loss per hour.) After you have done the 20 minute test in a number of homes, you will have a good idea of what houses are well insulated and which are not from your measurements.

Now if the house does really need improved insulation in the walls and ceilings, and better windows and doors, you can give the customer quotes on the improvements needed. If the customer agrees to have the work done, you will sign him to a contract, and then do the work yourself, or bring in your contractors to do the work required.

Here are some online calculators you can use to calculate home heat loss values, if you don't want to do your own calculations (but I think it is easier to do your own calculations):

http://www.builditsolar.com/References/Calculators/HeatLoss/HeatLoss.htm

http://www.shophmac.com/info-center/hvac-calculators/heat-load-calculator.php

I will not go into more details on this business, but be sure to read the general business requirements in the Appendix.

66. Home Inspection

Being a home inspector is a good business to get into. Usually, when a home is offered for sale, a prospective buyer will insist on a home inspection and correction of any faults. It is usually written into the contract at the insistence of a knowledgeable buyer (When you are buying a home, even a new one, you should insist on the home inspection condition and have it written into the contract.)
So what are the requirements to be a home inspector? You will need to get some education on home inspection, if you don't already have the required knowledge. Next, you will generally need to pass one or more exams and sometimes you have to be a member of some home inspection organization, such as the ASHI, or the NAHI. Some states allow certain other categories as sufficient for qualifications, such as an Architect, or a Structural Engineer.
You will also need to carry liability insurance in most states to be certified. Here is a link to the site for the Alabama state requirements:

http://www.ahit.com/training/stateregs/alabama_r
egs.cfm

You should research what is required in your
state or country.
How can you get the education and training to be
ready for your license? Here is a link to one site
of many as an example (I don't necessarily
recommend this company. You should do your
own research.)

http://www.homeinspectioninstitute.com/

What do home inspectors generally look for?
Mostly they love to find big things like a bad air
conditioning system, a worn out roof, bad or no
insulation in walls, attic, and crawl space, bad
plumbing or fixtures, and safety hazards.
Also, home inspectors look for other problems
too, such as un-grounded electrical outlets, loose
or bare wiring, lack of a hand railing on lengthy
steps, toilets that don't properly flush, plumbing
fixtures that don't work or leak, cracks in the
foundation, bad drainage, windows, doors,
heating and cooling efficiency, or anything that
needs repair.
To boost your business, you could also do home
appraisal work (see business no. 63), and home
insulation testing (see business no. 65.)
This should probably be enough work for a full-
time job in a medium or large sized urban
location. An another aspect to this work is to set

up a construction firm under your control that allows you to offer to the owner of the home that you can have all the necessary repairs done at a reasonable cost.

If the owner agrees, you bring in your contractors to do the work, and bill the owner accordingly. So you get additional business as a part of your home inspection job.

How should you advertise? Usually, the Yellow Pages, your own website, and direct marketing are the main ways to promote your business.

What do I mean by direct marketing? You need to contact real estate brokers in your area and let them know that you do home inspections. The brokers can then recommend your services to prospective buyers who want inspections done. Another marketing route is to talk to people you know are thinking about buying a home and let them know that you do inspections. Also contact any real estate investors you can find in your area and tell them you do home inspections.

When talking to real estate investors, you need to mention your competitive pricing, or that you will charge them less than any written quote they might have. Do your own research to find out the range of home inspection costs in your area, so that you know what to quote to be competitive.

I will not go into any more details on this business, but be sure to read the general business requirements in the Appendix.

67. Provide Services for the Elderly Citizens

Some seniors or elderly people need help with some simple tasks (other than in-home personal care.) What kinds of services? I will give you a few examples. Some elderly people do not need personal services in their home, but they don't drive a car anymore and maybe they can't walk very well, so they need help with things like shopping, transportation to the doctor, visiting relatives, going to church, or anything that requires them to leave their house and take care of some routine task.

One advantage of this business, is that once you have done some things for someone, they will probably call you for your help on an on-going basis. Well couldn't they take a cab? Maybe they could, but cabs are very expensive in some areas, and you could probably transport the person at a cheaper cost then a cab company that has a high overhead to pay for.

Also you can provide your customer with aid in walking or using a wheel chair, service that the cab driver might or might not provide. So how would you charge your customer? You should charge on a per-service basis, unless your customer is a steady user of your services, in which case you may offer your customer a flat monthly rate for your services. You have to be careful however, because one person could eat up your time with a lot of frivolous trips and activities.

How would you market your services? Older people are less likely to search for service on a computer or smart phone. They are more likely to use the *Yellow Pages*, or the newspaper to find someone to help them. Also you could distribute flyers with your business name, a short description of your services, and your telephone number, in areas where a lot of elderly people live.

Also tell all your friends, relatives, and acquaintances, that you are going into the elderly assistance service business. By the way don't let your relatives or friends talk you out of your plans, as they often try to do, no matter what you plan. Finally, this business can be a valuable service to the elderly community and rewarding work, if you are conscientious and perform your services with care, a smile, and respect for your customer.

I will not go into more details on this business, but be sure to read the general business requirements in the Appendix.

68. Home Sitting

This business is basically one of making arrangements between home owners and house sitters that you have vetted as responsible home sitters. How does it work? Someone who has a home (usually a large expensive home) will be away from their home for a relatively long time, maybe weeks or months, or they have the home for sale, wants someone to occupy and take care of the their home while they are away.

The important things for the owner of the home are that they want their home occupied for security reasons, but they don't want to pay a large amount of money to a guard service or some other expensive method of securing their home. They also want the people who occupy the house to be responsible, and to not damage the home or cause any problems in the home while the owner is away.

This is where you come in by providing home sitters, that you have previously verified to be responsible people, who will take good care of a home and the duties that might be associated with the job. To make money in the business, you must get a fee from the home owner or a membership fee from the home sitter that will do the work.

You could also be a home sitter yourself while you are operating your business. So why would you or your contractor sitters want to be a home sitter? First, you have a roof over your head and you don't have to pay someone rent on a residence while you are home sitting, especially if you have enough home sitting jobs on your calendar so that having a permanent residence is not necessary. If you own a home of your own, you could rent it out while you are home sitting. If you have a lease on an apartment, you might be able to sub-lease your apartment while you are away (before you sign a lease on a residence of some type, you should insist on the right to sub-lease the residence written into your lease agreement.) So the first advantage of home sitting for the sitter is saving on the cost of maintaining a residence. Secondly, if you willing to travel to different locations around the world to home sit, you will enjoy the vacation-like relaxed life (with some duties to take care of.)

So what are the problems with this business? You will have some potentially distasteful duties while home sitting, such as maintaining the lawn, walking the dogs (if any), and doing the house cleaning. The sitter needs to perform these duties responsibly to maintain his or her reputation as a responsible sitter. If you are home sitting yourself, your objective should be to line up home sitting jobs for yourself in advance so that you can go as quickly as possible from one job to the next one.

You will also be working to arrange jobs for your contractor sitters. Your contractor sitters will desire a solid schedule of jobs also, but you are not responsible for their job calendar, other than to try to arrange jobs for them when they are available. You will have to do this marketing work constantly even while you are home sitting to make sure you have the next job lined up.

You should request a reasonable fee from the owner for the sitting arranging for a sitter and to hold a certain time period open on your calendar in case the owner should cancel the sitting job. You will have to do some marketing research to find out what the going rates are in the business so that you will be competitive with other home sitting businesses. Here are some links to information on home sitting:

http://www.housesittingandmore.com/

http://www.housesittersamerica.com/

I will not go into any more details on this business, but be sure to read the general business requirements in the Appendix.

69. Interior Decorating

One advantage of being an interior decorator is that *in general* there are no requirements to be licensed in any state. There may be some towns or cities that may require a special license to be an interior decorator but usually and ordinary business license is sufficient. But be sure to check the requirements in your town or city. You should, however, become *certified* by some interior decorating organization.
Note that interior *design* does require college training and licensing because it may involve architectural work or changes. The following site is an example of a certifying organization for interior *decorating*:

http://www.cidinternational.org/aboutus.php

I don't necessarily recommend any particular certifying organization, however. You should do your own research to determine what organization you want to be certified by. Here is a site that offers training in interior decorating that I give only as an example of training that is available online.
You should contact a certifying organization to find out what kind of training they will accept for you to be certified before you sign up for any particular course:

http://www.scitraining.com/Interior_Decorating

So how does the business work? The first thing to do is to take the necessary training so you can be certified. You should know about the various styles of decorating that have been popular from the 1700's to the present. You can't predict in advance what a customer wants for decoration. It could be Early American, or the 1920's, or extreme modern decorating. The main secret to success in this business is to first know what kind of interior decorating the customer wants.
For example, someone is planning a retro style restaurant and he or she wants a 1950's style of decoration. You will have to be knowledgeable of the 50's period and the decorating styles that were in vogue at that time, for example. Or you may have a customer that wants a decoration change in their upscale apartment, but they can't

seem to give you a clear idea of what they really want.

They will rattle on about a lot of different ideas, but it is going to be hard to satisfy that customer. You will just have to listen closely and see if you can get some ideas to present later to the customer. In this case, tell the customer that you will go back to your office (or your home) and make some sketches of some of your ideas based on what the customer wants. You don't necessarily need artistic ability but you will need to be creative.

There is software you can obtain for your computer that could help, but I think the easiest way is to make hand drawings, or have someone assist you in making drawings, of say three or four ideas for the customer. You need at least three ideas so you have a chance of selling one of them to your customer, but don't present too much, and over-whelm, or confuse your customer. If the customer likes one of your ideas, and your fee is reasonable, you may get the job, or you may not.

You should learn some sales techniques for closing sales. You will have to be a combination of a good salesman and a creative decorator. You will also have to do some marketing to get jobs in the first place.

Word-of-mouth advertising is the best kind in this business, but to get started, first tell all your friends and acquaintances that you are going into this business, and you would pay a bounty for

any jobs they find for you, that result in a sale.
Then place some small advertisements in your
local newspaper.

This business will be best to operate in a large
city such as New York, Los Angeles, or Miami,
or large cities where there are upscale residences,
and business establishments, for example
restaurants that are potential customers for
decorating. I will not go into any more detail on
this business. You will know if you are really
interested in doing the decorating business or not.
 Be sure to read the general business
requirements in the Appendix.

70. Christmas Decorating

If you are looking for some part-time work that
you can do on week-ends to pick up some extra
money each year, maybe you can decorate homes
for the Christmas season (or whatever celebration
calls for home decorations during the year in
your area.)

Of course you need to be willing to climb ladders
to the roofs of houses, handle bulky items, and
usually untangle long strings of lights. Your most
likely customers will be people who either don't
have time to do the decorations themselves, or
don't want to do it themselves for whatever
reason.

The elderly home owners are sometimes potential
customers for you. The customer either provides
or pays for the lights. You charge for your time

placing the decorations and taking them back down again at the end of the holiday season. Be sure to charge your full amount for both placing and removing the decorations as soon as you have completed placing the decorations at the start of the season.

If the customer does not have any lights or decorations to provide to you, you can purchase the decorations for him or her and charge them according to your cost plus your time doing the shopping.

What is the most important aspect of this work? Creativity! If you can do a great job of decorating a customer's house, people will notice and you will get a good reputation for your work. People will start calling you and asking you to decorate their home. So how can you get started in this business?

You should place a small newspaper advertisement before the start of the season and continue to run it into the start of the season. Also you could place flyers in up-scale neighborhoods where you are more likely to find customers. Also to get started, you should be very competitive in your pricing. Do some research to find out what the going prices are in your area for decorating homes.

Get some quotes from decorators on your own house. That will give you an idea of how much to charge your customers. Make sure you get a business license and good liability insurance as well as a personal injury policy for yourself.

Make sure that your liability insurance protects yourself from damages to property and protects you against lawsuits against you by your contractors that help you (if any), and the home owner.

Once you began to have a lot of people calling you to decorate their homes, you will have to have some tight scheduling to get all the work done in time. So to hold a time slot for decoration job open, you may have to ask the customer to give you a deposit in case he or she should cancel later.

I will not go into more details on this business, but be sure to read the general business requirements in the Appendix.

71. Publish Books Online

You can write books and publish them yourself online as either e-books (electronic books), a hard cover book, or both. How do you make money in this business? You publish your book using the services of an online book vendor such as *Amazon* or *Barnes & Noble*. Both are good, but it is easier to publish on Amazon, I have found, especially if you are doing the e-books. You can make money in e-books if you are a good writer and your books become popular. If you are just starting out with writing, it may take a long time to become recognized and have significant sales volume. The main secrets to being successful are to

1) make sure your title has good keywords in it so that people will be more likely to find your book when they do searches.
Use the Google Keyword Search Tool to check your titles to see what the probability is that people are searching for a word or phrase that is in the title of your book.
2) If you know of a book similar to yours that is popular, or a hot movie title, you might make your title similar to it.
For example, there is a movie with the title *Contraband.* So the title of your book could be *Contraband Cargo*, or something containing the word contraband. But before you give your book its title, make sure you do a search to determine if another book has the same exact title that you have chosen. If so, change your title a little bit, so it will not be confused with the other book.
3) Make sure you use good keywords in your book description also.
4) If you are writing a novel of some kind, you should have some interesting action or event taking place that will grab and hold the reader's attention. This is especially important because vendors like Amazon and Barnes & Noble, allow the potential buyer to view the first few pages of a book using the "look inside feature" on their website.
5) You should prepare an interesting and professional looking cover. You may have to engage an artist to create your cover unless you have good artistic ability.

So how can you get started? Let's suppose that you are starting out with an e-book. Further suppose that you have decided to publish on the Amazon Kindle platform. The website you need is a little hard to find so I show the link below. This site gives you a step-by-step process to publish your book. First you will have to create an account and provide your correct name, address, and tax-payer identification number.

On the Amazon system you upload Microsoft Word documents and Amazon will automatically convert your document to the Kindle format. You can upload all of your information and a picture of the cover of your book. You can set your own price and select either a 30% or 70% commission payment, subject to Amazon's rules and limitations.

Amazon will automatically calculate the conversions of your price into various foreign currencies and translate your book into other major languages automatically. It may take several days to get your book 'live' and published on-line. If after it has been published, you want to change something, you can do an edit and re-submit it, or you can un-publish it for any reason to cancel it or make major changes, like changing the title.

Although you have to use your real name when creating your account, you can use any name you want to for the author's name. So the author's name could be a pen name, or even the name of a real person(s) (if you have the real person's authority to do so), or yourself, of course. Here is the Amazon website:

https://kdp.amazon.com/self-publishing/signin

Make sure you read the Terms and Conditions carefully. Note that once you have published a book with one publisher, such as Amazon, the publisher has exclusive rights to the document and you cannot publish the same document with another publisher. However, you may publish some books with one publisher and other books with other publishers, as long as you don't give exclusive rights to all of your works to one publisher (don't ever do that.)

If you want to publish a hard back version of your book there are some sites that will help you publish your book for a small fee. You can then order some copies for yourself and get it listed on Amazon or with another publisher. The company will then print your book on a per order basis from customers in quantities of one or more. Their process is electronically automated so that they don't have to print a large run as in the traditional way. Here is the Amazon site that gives you information about their affiliate that will produce your hardback book:

https://www.amazon.com/gp/seller-account/mm-product-page.html?topic=200354160&ld=AZOnDemand
MakeM

If you want to publish an e-book on the Barnes & Noble Nook, it is a similar procedure but it is a little more difficult. Whatever format you use to write your book, you will have to get it into a .lit electronic form before you can submit it to Nook. Also Barnes & Noble requires a lot of personal information that you will have to give if you want to publish on Nook. If you are determined to publish on Nook, here is the website to get started with:

http://www.pubit.com

Otherwise the same comments I mentioned above concerning keywords in titles and descriptions apply on the Nook also.
 I will not go into more details on this business, but be sure to read the general business requirements in the Appendix.

72. Heating, Ventilation, and Air Conditioning
If you have mechanical ability and you don't mind doing some physical work, you might be interested in HVAC work.
To be a HVAC technician you don't generally need to be licensed. But to run your own HVAC contracting business, you will usually need to have certification by the state you are operating in. But some states only require that you have a certificate of completion of a HVAC course from

an accredited HVAC training school. There are lots of HVAC schools.

You need to make sure you go to a legitimate accredited school so you don't waste your time and money. Here is a link to an online school, but be sure to do your own search and selection (I don't necessarily recommend this particular school.)

http://www.onlineschools.org/online-HVAC-training-programs/

It will take you anywhere from 6 months to two years to get your certificate, so make sure you find out ahead of time what the length of the course will be. Some companies advertise a 2 week course.

But don't be fooled, such outfits are usually not accredited.

The HVAC business is a good one if you can get your business established in your area.

But it will not be easy. You will need a truck and probably an assistant (as a contractor to you.)

You should advertise in the Yellow Pages and in your local newspaper. If you have a panel truck, you should have it painted with your business name, logo, your telephone number, and your website name if you have one.

Otherwise do not spend a lot of money on advertising until you have sufficient revenue to cover it plus your expenses. Your advertising will consist mainly of word-of-mouth. If you do a great job, you are more likely to get repeat business and calls from other people who hear that you do good work. Initially, you will probably do mostly service work. But you should have one or more sources of HVAC new equipment to sell to your customer if he or she needs a new system.

Eventually, as your business increases, your main source of revenue will be the sale of new HVAC equipment as well as service work. That should be your goal to grow your number of customers and your revenue. If you are good at this kind of work and make the right decisions, you have the potential to create a million dollar business. One key to your success will be to contract highly skilled and responsible technicians that will do good installation and service work.

This is very important because you will be busy managing your business and you will not have time to go on service runs to supervise jobs. Another problem you will have to deal with is that you must be willing to provide 24 hour service seven days a week. Of course you can charge premium time for work done outside of regular hours. One more thing, make sure that the brand(s) of HVAC units you sell are the best in quality and reliability for the price.

I will not go into more details on this business, but be sure to read the general business requirements in the Appendix.

73. Repair Lawn Mowers

If you are mechanically inclined, you may be good at small engine repair work. Who would be the potential customers? Anyone who has to take care of a lawn. How much money can you make doing it? An average repair bill is around $125, more or less. If you can do two repairs a day, that is a gross revenue of $1500 for a 6-day week. My idea for this business is to do mobile repair-- that is you go to the customer's home to repair the mower on-site. By doing business this way you don't have to have a brick and mortar store, and you don't have to invest or borrow a lot of money at the start of your business.

It also saves the customer a lot of effort as he or she does not have to haul the mower to a repair store. It is especially helpful to the customer if he or she has a riding mower that is a lot more difficult to transport to a repair shop.

Of course you should have a minimum charge for a home visit, in the case that the customer's machine does not really need repair, or the customer tells you he has changed his mind when you arrive at his location. Be sure to advise the customer about the minimum charge for a visit on your first contact.

If you do a good job, you may get repeat business from the same customer as well as calls from other people that hear by word-of-mouth that you do good work. In this business you would look more professional if you have a panel truck with your business name and phone number painted on the truck.

The truck will also be a good way to transport your tools and carry a loaner mower that the customer can use if you have to take the customer's mower to a repair shop for some major work that is not practical to do on site. Another aspect to this business is the possibility to sell a customer a new mower if he needs one. You could even haul one or two new mowers with you in your truck to have available for sale to the customer. So how would you get started? First of all make sure that you know how to repair small engines. If you don't have a lot of experience, it might be a good idea to get a job at a small engine repair shop for a few months or until you feel confident enough to start your own operation.

How should you advertise? Be careful in advertising your business. Don't advertise your rates as competition could under-quote you. If a customer asks for a quote, only give him a verbal quote and make sure the customer knows that your quote is an estimate only and the total cost depends on what is actually wrong with the mower that needs repair. A good place to advertise is the Yellow Pages.

Once you get a good business going, you might want to have more trucks out doing work for you. Make sure you contract only highly skilled people to work for you.

I will not go into more details on this business, but be sure to read the general business requirements in the Appendix.

74. Life Insurance Agent

Being an insurance agent may seem like working for someone else, which is true in the sense that the insurance company gets the largest share of the customer's payments.
But you work for yourself in the sense that the more insurance you can sell, the more your residual payments will be, and you will have an income from the residuals even after you retire.
If you are a really good salesman it is possible to become a millionaire, but it will take a lot of hard work and a long time to achieve this goal. How does it work? You develop leads on potential customers for life insurance and call to make appointments with the people to explain your company's insurance plans.
You may have charts with graphs showing the advantages of each of your insurance plans vs. other forms of investments such as US treasury bonds. There are two main forms of life insurance, 'whole life' and 'term' insurance. The 'term' insurance plans are cheaper but the customer cannot accumulate a cash value with it and can never withdraw money from the plan. It does not pay any interest either.
On the other hand, 'whole life' plan provides you with dividends and an accumulation of cash

value from which you can draw on in an
emergency, or withdraw when you no longer
need the policy. The 'term' insurance plan
usually drops to zero value at age 65 or 70
whereas the whole life plan is good for life. You
should work with a well known life insurance
company such as New York Life, Prudential, etc.
This is important to get the attention of a
potential customer when you first contact him.
You must become known in your community by
people who are in a position to buy life insurance
and have a family to support. A single person
does not really need life insurance. A married
man needs to think about support for his wife and
children in the event of his untimely death. So
how do you get leads on potential customers?
One way is to join some civic organizations such
as the Rotary, Lions, Kiwanis, and others.
Whatever organizations you join, you must be
active and help support the charitable activities
that the organization is involved in.
As you meet people in the organizations be sure
to give them one of your insurance business cards
and tell them you are looking for people who are
interested in buying a life insurance policy. Also
be alert to the needs of your next door neighbor
or someone you meet in the course of everyday
life.
You never know where a sale might come from
or who will buy a policy from you. In this
business you will have to have a lot of patience
as you will have to talk to a lot of people and

make a lot of presentations just to make a few sales. But if you sell a one million dollar policy to someone, your commission will be substantial. Before you sign with any particular company, make sure you know what your sales commission rate will be and what other benefits the company provides. One advantage of selling life insurance is that you are your own boss to a large extent and you don't have to establish a business and take care of all the legal requirements that go with it.

If you are very good at selling insurance and you become the top salesman in the local office, you may be promoted to the position of branch manager. In this position you will still receive residuals from the sales you have made as well as receiving a percentage of the all of the sales that the other salesmen in the office make.

So that is a very lucrative position to have. I will not go into more details on this business, but be sure to research all of the aspects of the insurance sales business and think hard before you decide to become an insurance salesman.

75. Make Money out of Junk

There is an old saying: "One man's trash is another man's treasure." If you have ever cruised through a 'well-to-do' neighborhood on a night before trash pick-up, and on Saturday night after a lot of people have cleaned out their garage, you see various items placed out on the curb to be picked up by the trash men.

Most of the junk put on the curb seems useless. But look at it from the point of view of someone who knows how to find value out of junk. For example, often you will see water heaters out on the curb. The water heater usually has an aluminum outer sheath, a steel tank, and often still has copper fittings and copper pipes still attached to the hot and cold water connections. So what can you do with that?

If you collect a number of these tanks, you can disassemble them and sort out the metals into piles of aluminum, steel, and copper. Once you have significant amounts, take them to a metals recycler. You will receive money for the metals. The following links will allow you to get an idea of spot scrap metal prices (Your local recycler will have his own prices, so ask what rates he is quoting before you load up your truck and drive to his location to sell your metals.)

http://www.metalprices.com/dailysnapshots/Index

http://www.earthworksrecycling.com/index.html

The first link above gives you prices for refined metals. The second site is a typical local recycler. You will note that the prices of a local recycler are usually a lot lower than the refined metal prices.

As I am writing this book, some typical scrap metal prices are approximately as follows (but you should do your own research):

Iron and steel $0.25 per pound
Aluminum $0.80 per pound
Copper $2.35 per pound
Car batteries $9

Note that the prices a recycler will quote you depend on the condition of the scrap. For example, if you have carefully separated copper so that it does not contain other junk, you will get a better price for your load. Painted aluminum is not as valuable as clean aluminum, and so forth. What else can you get money for out of junk? Often people throw out old appliances such as washing machines, dryers, and refrigerators. Of course, usually they are not in working order, but often can be made to work with some repairs. Other items that show up on curbs are furniture, cardboard boxes, scrap wood, television sets, old computers, and a lot of other things.
Electronic circuit boards and re-chargeable batteries can be recycled to recover copper, gold, silver, palladium, platinum, and valuable rare earth metals. Here is a link to a typical electronic scrap recycler. I don't necessarily recommend this site. Be sure to do your own research:

http://cashforelectronicscrapusa.com/what-we-buy/high-grade-boards/

Much of the ordinary junk you can find on the curb, can be recycled, repaired, or even just cleaned up to be a saleable item. You will need the space, preferably an indoor area or warehouse to store and sell the better items that you have repaired to sell. So the main things you need in this business are a pick-up truck and a place to store items that will not result in complaints from your neighbors or your local government officials.

A little more ambitious related business is the traditional automobile junk yard. This is also a good business because you can not only sell scrap metal, but you can sell used automobile parts of various kinds for good prices, especially if the parts are rare or hard to find.

An even more ambitious business, is to become a recycler yourself. If you are brave enough to tackle a recycling business, the best one to get into is recycling of electronic scrap and other types of precious metal scrap, to recover the precious metals.

However, you will find that a lot of equipment will be required and you will have to deal with very severe environmental requirements, whether you use chemical recovery methods or a smelting process. Anything you do that might pollute the air or water systems is very expensive and difficult to deal with.

I will not go into more details on the junk business, but be sure to read the general business requirements in the Appendix.

76. Lawn Cut and Trim

What can you do if you have a pick-up truck with a trailer, a riding lawn mower, and a 'weed wacker'? Well, you can cut and trim lawns. How much money can you make? As I write this book the average price for cutting a lawn is $50 per cut and trim. In the growing season (or in some areas, year-round), the average yard will need to be cut about every ten days.

So you could collect $150 per month for each yard you cut and trim. If you can build your business to do 20 yards a month (cutting and trimming a yard on each of the 5 working days per week), your income would be $3000 per month or $36000 per year before taxes. Not a bad income for a simple business. If you do a good job and you get enough customers by word-of-mouth advertising, and canvassing neighborhoods for business, maybe you can cut and trim two lawns per working day, or $6000 per month, equivalent to $72,000 on a yearly basis before taxes.

Now let's say you have built your business up to the point where you could do 80 lawns per month, or four per working day. But you would have to work very hard to do four per day yourself. So how could you handle so much business? You could have two crews of two men each. You have equipment for each crew to use. It would be easiest if you had two pick-up trucks and two trailers.

You would assign each crew to do two lawns per day. Use only contract labor. Let's say that you pay each man of each crew $10, or 20% of the price for each lawn they cut and trim. You then collect a net average of $30 per lawn, or $7200 per month before taxes. We see a law of diminishing returns setting in when you have to pay labor costs. It may not be advantageous to hire contract labor to do more lawns.

But if you are willing to do the work yourself, it would make a great part-time income for little investment, especially if you already own a pick-up truck and a good mower.

I will not go into more details on this business, but be sure to read the general business requirements in the Appendix.

77. Lawn Weed and Feed

The lawn weed and feed business is a good one but I don't recommend signing up for an expensive franchise. Instead you can buy your own equipment and obtain the chemicals you need to do the job. There are two ways to go. One is to buy small fertilizer feeders and spray tanks that you carry around by hand, or you can buy a truck designed for the purpose. If you can get a truck for the purpose, you will look more professional to the customer and you can do your work easier and faster. There are already used trucks available for sale. This is a link to find trucks:

http://www.commercialtrucktrader.com/

Your search for a truck would be a 'spray truck'. Of course the newer it is and the more useful it is, the more expensive it will be. If you shop around you may be able to find one that will serve the purpose at a reasonable price.
The following is a link for spray equipment for manual application and equipment you could mount on a truck bed:

http://www.nationwidewholesaledirect.com/fimc o_sprayers.html?gclid=CMXMyNTF27ACFYeo 4AodSnbM1w

Also you will need a source of chemicals and you will need to buy the chemicals in bulk at wholesale prices to keep your costs under control. The following is a link to sources of herbicides.
Note that you must use a selective herbicide that will not kill both grass and weeds. You should buy only concentrate that you mix with water in your spray tank to cover large areas.

http://www.nextag.com/wholesale-herbicide/shop-html?nxtg=27400a28050c-9F64805415FFC7F8

You will also need a wholesale source of fertilizer. You will need to shop for wholesale fertilizers. Here is a link to a basic supplier of fertilizers as a starting point:

http://www.adm.com/en-US/products/industrial/fertilizers/Pages/default.aspx

Here is the creative part of the business. You can come up with your own mixtures or combinations of herbicides and fertilizers that will make lawns look beautiful. When mixing and applying the chemicals, make sure you follow the instructions that come with the chemicals to avoid creating a health hazard or ruining a lawn.
Experiment on small patches of your own lawn with different combinations to see what works best. Note that different grasses may require different kinds of fertilizers and different lawns have different kinds of weeds to contend with. You will have to do your own research to develop the best techniques.
Your marketing plan will be similar to the business described above, 'Lawn Cut and Trim'. I will not go into more details on this business,

but be sure to read the general business requirements in the Appendix.

78. Be a Gardner

No I am not talking about planting lilies in someone's backyard. I am talking about heavy duty garden development from scratch, under the direction of the customer or a landscape architect. You may also do some small jobs, cultivating, pruning, or planting for a customer.
real money will be in building or creating new gardens. So what kind of equipment will you need? You need at least a large pick-up truck, some garden hand tools, shovels, a rotor-tiller, a wheel barrel, a pick-ax, a regular ax, a chain saw, and so forth. A dump truck would be very good for hauling large loads of dirt and debris from 'tear out' jobs. Trucks do not have to be new, of course.
You also may occasionally need an air hammer with an air compressor, to break up old concrete patios or driveways. The air hammer and compressor can be rented if you need one on a certain job. You may also need some other heavier power equipment that you would rent on a day-today basis, such as a back-hoe, a post-hole digger, and a small bull dozer. Also, you may need to do some tree removal or trimming.
If you don't want to do the tree work yourself, or any dangerous or difficult work, you should hire a contractor to do that part of the work. A good

example of this is pouring and smoothing out wet concrete. You would probably hire a concrete contractor for that kind of work.

Also you would be wasting your valuable time if you try to do a lot of the 'grunt' work yourself when you could be working on getting new jobs lined up. Also for a lot of 'grunt' work you would sign up some contract labor. You are a business man doing garden design and construction as a contractor, not a 'grunt' laborer.

But before you start this business, you need to know something about gardening, and the characteristics of typical landscaping plants, flowers, shrubs, and trees. What kinds of things do you need to know? I will give you only a short list here and you will have to do your own research, if you are not already knowledgeable in the field:

1) Learn what kinds of shrubs, plants, and trees are typically used in landscape gardens.

2) Find out what kinds are suitable for the climate of the area.

3) Learn when to plant each kind of plant.

4) Learn how to plant each kind of plant. How big a hole? How deep? What kind of soil?

5) Learn what fertilizers to use for each kind of plant.

6) Learn how to water plants.

7) Learn how to control pests. Learn how to use pesticide and organic control methods.

8) Learn how to care for and maintain a garden.

9) Learn how to design gardens and landscape layouts yourself.

10) Learn how to design patios, decks, and walkways.

You may have to do research, read some books, or find online information.

So how would you market your skills? There are two main routes to getting work in this business. First you would contact landscape architects in your area and try to get contracts to do work for them.

In order to get their work, you will have to quote very competitively and be ready to work on their time schedule. Second, you can market your services directly to customers through a web site, flyers distributed in good neighborhoods, and word-of-mouth advertising.

Get business cards made, and talk to your friends and acquaintances about your new business. You should also join some service clubs such as the Rotary, the Kiwanis, and as many others, as you can handle, to promote your business to members.

I will not go into more detail on this business, but be sure to read the general business requirements in the Appendix.

79. Online Media Store

If you have a lot of books, movie DVDs, music CDs, tapes, or even vinyl records, you might have enough to start an online store. Some old or rare items can be worth a lot of money. For example, a copy of Frank Sinatra's album "Come Fly With Me" in the original vinyl can be worth up to $1000.

Good items are old or rare books, VHS tapes, vinyl records, and even certain DVDs and CDs that have become rare. Also you can go to the local mission stores and find piles of old books, records, VHS tapes, and so forth for very low prices. A vinyl record can sell for $0.50 or $1.00 even though it might really be worth a lot more. I have found some old vinyl records, old shellac 78 RPM records, and even old 45's, that are in perfect condition that I only paid $0.50 for. I bought a rare book signed by its author for $0.25 that is worth about $75 as I write this book.

When you sell your item you can judge the price you charge by looking for pricing on an identical item that someone else is selling online.

An easy way to do that is to look it up on Amazon.com. Of course, when you sell an item online you also charge extra for shipping. So how would you get this business started? The first step is to read the general business requirements in the Appendix. Next get your own website set up.

You can use an existing website like Volusion.com that will assist you in setting up your online store with all the features you need such as the ability to process credit cards, and so forth. Once you get your site up and running, you sell your items direct to customers using online advertising on sites like Facebook and Google.

Another good thing to do is to partner with one or more online retailers.

A good retailer is Amazon because when someone searches for an item, if you have it, Amazon will list your store in their search results. Your site will not be listed directly, but because your item is used, it will be listed under the category 'used'. Let's assume that you have an original vinyl copy of Frank Sinatra's album "Come Fly with Me." Here is the link that shows the result of a search on Amazon for the album:

http://www.amazon.com/Come-Fly-Vinyl-Frank-Sinatra/dp/B0030BOCJG/ref=sr_1_9?ie=UTF8&qid=1340573584&sr=8-9&keywords=come+fly+with+me+frank+sinatra

From the same site I can look up the used item:

http://www.amazon.com/gp/offer-listing/B0030BOCJG/ref=dp_olp_used?ie=UTF8&condition=used

Now you see the used rare item listed for $999, as I am writing this book.

In this business you must be very competitive on price. You will be rated on your service, accuracy, ease of returning items, time to delivery, and personal service by telephone when a customer wants it. Remember the credo, "The customer is always right."

If you check some of the retailers that partner with Amazon on the Amazon site, you will find that vendors have various ratings, some low, and some very high such as above 99%. You will also see the statistic of how many orders that the vendor processed for that rating.

Items also have written reviews that customers have written, pro and con. You always need to state exactly what the condition of the item is, including a description of defects, if any, so the customer does not feel cheated when he receives an item in sub-standard condition when you advertised the item as 'excellent' or 'very good'. As you gain more experience in your business, you may find places to buy new un-used items at lower than market prices. Always make sure your shipping and handling cost is correct. Add a little to the shipping and handling cost you charge the customer to be on the safe side. Make sure the item is properly packaged so that it does not get damaged in shipping.

I will not go into more detail on this business, but be sure that you read the general business requirements in the Appendix.

80. Be a Picker

Probably almost everyone has seen the television show "Pickers". Is picking a legitimate business? Yes. Can you make money doing it? Yes, if you are good at judging the value of various items based on their rarity, condition, and the possibility of re-selling the item at a profit, or trading it for something better.

But there is a degree of uncertainty in this business that you should think about. Suppose you buy an item that looks like it is a good buy. Maybe it is a good buy, but how long will it take to re-sell it? How much can you really sell it for? It could be worth a lot less than what you think it is worth, unless you are expert in the value of such items.

While you are waiting to re-sell the item, you may have a significant amount of money tied up in it. Your investment is not earning interest and you probably can't afford to wait until the item becomes even more rare and valuable.

So was it really a good buy, or could you have used your money more wisely to buy something that has a hot market and you can re-sell quickly? On the other hand, if you are a sharp buyer, know what items you want that sell good, and you are able to haggle with the seller until you can buy the item at a very good price, you could be very successful in this business. You will know if you are that person or not.

So where can you find good items to pick from? Usually you will find items in the country. Good areas are where there are a lot of small farms such as eastern Tennessee, the Midwest, North and South Dakota, and other states that have rural areas. You will need to do a lot of travel through the countryside, and a lot of research.

If you know what kinds of items you are looking for, this will help you to narrow your search. For example, if you are looking for old cars and trucks in good condition, concentrate on the Sothern states, and the West in arid states such as South Dakota, Arizona, New Mexico, and California. Vehicles in the North are usually rusted due to salt put on the streets to melt ice in the wintertime. The automobiles tend to be in better condition in arid areas due to the low humidity.

Also you may find items such as old gasoline pumps, metal signs, and other items made out of iron are in better condition in the arid states. Some people go picking just because they want to collect the items they love. That is all right, but if you are trying to do it for a business, you need to stay as unemotional as possible about what items you deal with but be as expert as possible in what items are hot and easy to sell.

Of course, you never want to tip off the seller that you really want something bad. Always act like a reluctant buyer and offer ridiculously low prices to start with. Know in advance the maximum amount of money you are willing to spend on an item. If you can't get your price, just say no.

Remember the credo, 'buy low and sell high'. But this does not mean that you can't enjoy your work and have fun. Always be friendly and never make derogatory comments on what the seller has to offer. Remember that part of the business is to make good contacts, friends, and find good sources of items to pick from.

Sometimes a seller will refer you to another seller if you are looking for a certain item that he does not have. So always ask; "Do you know of anyone else that might have the item I am looking for?" If you are looking for more expensive items, like automobiles, boats, etc., you may be able to find what you want by doing a search on the internet.

A great number of automobiles and trucks are advertised for sale on the internet, from old classics to new cars and trucks. You can narrow your search criteria and quickly find what you are looking for.

You will also get a good idea what a certain vehicle is worth based on the listings you see online. The following is a link to popular automobile search website:

http://www.edmunds.com/used-cars/

I will not go into more details on this business, but be sure to read the general business requirements in the Appendix.

81. Writing Apps for the iPhone or Android Cell Phones

If you have a technical bent, or have some computer programming knowledge, you my be able to write "apps" (applications) for either the iPhone or Android based cell phones, or both. For the iPhone there is a programming system called iOS.

There is a lot of information on the internet on programming mobile devices for both the iPhone and the Android system. The iOS programming language for the iPhone is somewhat like the "C" programming language, but looks like a collection of short English phrases.

The following link gives you a good idea how to get started for iPhone app programming:

http://www.switchonthecode.com/tutorials/an-absolute-beginners-guide-to-iphone-development

You should note that Apple has to approve all apps for its iPhone before an app can be released. On the other hand, the Android system is an open system and you don't have to get approval to submit your app. But you do always need to make sure your app is reliable and does not violate FCC decency requirements.

App code for the Android System is based on the Java coding system and it is more like "C" code. But don't be afraid to tackle the job and learn how to do it. The following link is a good explanation of how to get started:

http://www.makeuseof.com/tag/write-google-android-application/

So what makes writing apps for cell phones a business? Because you can make a lot of money if you develop a popular app. The risk to you is practically nothing except spending some time learning how to program the apps and get them approved (for the iPhone) and marketed.

So how do you market your app? For the iPhone, you need to work with Apple. The following link will get you help from Apple to market your app:

http://advertising.apple.com/developers/?cid=wwa-naus-seg-iaddev100604-000001&cp=appadvertising&sr=sem

To market an Android app, you might be more successful if you follow the Google system. The following link gives you the information you need to work with Google to market your app:

http://developer.android.com/distribute/googleplay/publish/preparing.html

As I write this book, Google has just released their Nexus 7 tablet computer, and guess what? It uses the Android system. So there will be lots of opportunity to develop apps for this system.

Also, don't forget about Facebook with almost 1 billion users. People are writing apps that can be loaded onto your Facebook page so all you have to do is click on them. These apps will work on smart phones, tablets, or laptop computers.

There are already thousands of apps that have been programmed and made available to smart cell phones, iPads, and other tablet computers.

There is still a lot of opportunity in the apps development business. So if you have a good idea for an app, don't be afraid to develop it. You will know if this business is for you or not. I will not go into more detail on this business, but be sure to read the general business requirements in the Appendix.

82. Pet Grooming

Have fun at this job. What exactly you have to do is a little fuzzy. But there is a lot of money in the work if you do a good job and satisfy your customers. It is a simple business. You can run it from a brick-and-mortar store or you can do it from a mobile van such as a converted motorized mobile home that you drive to the customer's premises to groom their pets.

The mobile service is usually more convenient for the customer. So how do you get started in this business? Of course, the first thing is to decide on your place of business, brick-and-mortar, or mobile. Start preparing your work area and tools. You will need tables to place the pets on, shavers, shears, brushes, combs, etc.

When you are getting close to opening your business, start promoting your business. Tell all your friends and acquaintances that you are going into the pet grooming business and start your advertising program. Don't spend a lot of money on advertising. Run small advertisements in the newspaper.

Build a website (or have someone build it for you.) Print cards that you can put on bulletin boards at pet stores. Talk to pet store managers and arrange for them to refer customers to you (for a percentage of your billing.) Your business will be built primarily on word-of-mouth advertising.

Don't go into this business unless you love animals and you are willing to put up with the different characteristics of different pets. Your primary business will be grooming dogs, such poodles, and other long hair dogs. Someone may bring in a show dog for grooming and you need to be knowledgeable in the different ways that show dogs are groomed. Always find out exactly what kind of grooming each customer wants. You may keep a photo album of dogs that you have groomed so you can show the customer in case the customer does not know how the dog should be groomed.

You must also have patience in this business. Never approach an animal too quickly or handle them roughly. If you scare a dog or treat it roughly you may be setting yourself up for a good bite. So be patient, careful, and loving with each animal you groom. If you do the grooming correctly, the animal may even enjoy the process and this almost guarantees repeat business with the customer.

Invite the customer to stay and watch the animal getting groomed. This is your chance to get to know the customer and possibly even make friends with him or her.

I will not go into more detail on this business, but be sure to read the general business requirements in the Appendix.

83. Photograph Weddings

There is money in wedding photography, or what I call social photography. That is, you concentrate on social events or social photography services, such as weddings, model photo-shoots, baby pictures, school pictures (yearly pictures, graduation, proms, etc.) little league photos, family portraits, parades, parties, service club events, and other events too numerous to mention here.

You should be able to do quality still shots as well as high definition video. But you can start with still shots until you build your business. You will need a quality digital camera, such as a Nikon, or a Cannon in the professional series. You will not make much of an impression with a small pocket camera, no matter how good it makes photos.

You should also have good flash equipment and other lighting equipment so you can get good pictures in poor lighting conditions. Churches, where most weddings are performed, usually do not have very good lighting.

Remember that full sunlight is the best lighting you can get, so always suggest outdoor pictures, especially for groups if the weather is good and the sun is shining. Once you have taken your pictures, be sure to do any corrections or cropping that is needed on your computer. Photoshop software is good for the job. If you don't have a color laser printer to print your photos, you may be better off getting your photos printed by a professional photo service that will give you a good discount from retail prices.

When you are first starting out with this business, you should make sure your prices are competitive with other photographers, or even bargain priced for your area, so you can attract more customers and get your business started fast.

So how do you advertise? First of all, set up a good website and incorporate plenty of good keywords so it will have a chance of showing up when someone does a search on Google or other search engines. Also some small advertisements on online classifieds, and in local newspapers and magazines, will help.

Go to home shows and set up a booth with samples of your work. Get business cards printed and pass out to your friends. Also get your cards inside wedding dress shops, boutiques, and wherever women shop for clothes. Stick with the small shops and introduce yourself to the owner or people that work there. Join some major service clubs such as the Rotary and Kiwanis. Be active in the clubs and get your name known. Always pass out your business card to your friends, acquaintances, and any new people you meet. You don't need a brick and mortar store to start with, as long as you do work outside your home. You may be able to set up a studio in your home, depending on local laws.

I will not go into more details on this business, but be sure to read the general business requirements in the Appendix.

84. Freelance Photography

What is 'freelance photography'? It is almost any photography that you can make money on, but here I am not talking about weddings or family pictures, I am talking about pictures and videos that are professional quality and good enough to sell to newspapers, magazines, television stations.

You may work under contract for awhile to a certain media outlet where you have specific assignments, for example, war coverage, human interest, disaster scenes, sporting events, photographing models for catalogs, and other photography assignments. Or you may work without a contract, photographing, scenes or events that you think you can sell to media outlets.

Great pictures and videos that no one else obtained but you, can be worth big bucks. But on the other hand, you could work for a year or more by yourself and not produce anything saleable. Personally I think that unless you become famous for your work, you are better off to work on a contract basis. But remember, if you become an employee for someone, then you are no longer freelance and it is very likely that you will not make as much money.

As a freelance photographer, you can pick your jobs and name your prices. But of course, you need to be competitive with other freelance photographers. You may have to do a little detective work to find out what other freelancers charge so you can quote reasonable prices.

The main element in this work to be successful, is to obtain unusual pictures and videos of the highest professional quality. You must have equipment that is equal to the job. How will you market your services? Get business cards printed. Get a 'press' badge from a photography association or get one from an online service that will make one for you. Here is an online company that will make you a photo badge with your own design.

http://www.create-a-badge.com/

Your badge is very important to get you into places and situations that you might not otherwise be allowed into. Make sure your badge says 'PRESS' in large caps. It should also have your photo, name, your business name, address, and phone number. Make sure you have an answering service or someone who will answer your number, confirm your identity, and that you work for *Eastern News Service*, or what ever your business name is, (in case someone decides to check on you.) Make your business name sound like a big media company.

Get out of the house and start taking pictures. Find some tornados to photograph, storm damage, natural disasters, or anything that will make spectacular pictures.

Make a portfolio showing your best photography work that you have, and start canvassing your local media outlets. Also send letters to major magazine editors with one or two samples of your photos. Telephone editors and tell them what you do and find out if they are interested in seeing your work. Advertise online and small ads in newspapers and magazines.

It will not be easy to get started. It will take a lot of shoe leather, phone calls, and letter writing. You will know if this business is for you or not. I will not go into more details on this business, but be sure to read the general business requirements in the Appendix.

85. Pan for Gold

If you are retired, you want a relaxing simple business, and you like to be outdoors, maybe you might like to pan for gold. To do this kind of work, you will need a lot of patience. But you don't need a lot of equipment.

All you need is a good location in an area where it is known that gold can be found, a small stream, a pan, and maybe some screens that are used to filter out ordinary rocks and expose the gold dust or an occasional nugget (if you are very lucky.) Some people get fancier and build a 'sluice' to run water through and filter out the gold. You will need a good map, a compass, a good hat, and plenty of water to drink.

If you are staying all day in the field, you should have food packed with you so that you do not get weak. Salt tablets are good to have so that the salt level in your body does not drop too low. This activity can be performed anytime the weather is good and your stream is flowing.

The basic panning technique is to dip your pan into the sand or silt at the bottom of the stream, bring up a small quantity, and then gradually shake out the bulk of the material until you see the black specks of fine gold, or the sparkle of the larger particles, in the bottom of the pan. Gold is much heavier than dirt or sand, so it sinks to the bottom of the pan. The technique is best performed in sunshine so that you can see the sparkle of the large grains of gold dust. Pour out the small particles of gold into a jar or other container that they will not leak out of and that you will not lose.

If you get a little dirt in the collection container don't worry about it. You can clean it later by various techniques (see the website links below.)

http://imnh.isu.edu/digitalatlas/teach/lsnplns/gold pnlp.htm

http://www.ehow.com/how_5201475_use-jet-dry-gold-refining.html

http://www.finishing.com/200/33-2.shtml

So where can you find gold? There are a lot of places like California, Oregon, Arizona, etc. You can do some searches on the Internet to find various places. Here are some links that have general locations information:

http://ezinearticles.com/?8-Best-Places-to-Pan-For-Gold&id=2391641

So you have collected gold dust, how do you get it changed into money? Once you have say 5 ounces of gold dust or more, you should first get it assayed at a reliable company. An assay will determine how much pure gold is in your collection of gold dust.

As I write this book, gold is about $1620 per ounce in the refined and purified state. Five ounces of pure gold should be worth about $8000. You will not get that much for your gold dust, but you should get a price that is a good percentage of the refined value of gold, depending on how much gold is in your dust. Here are some links for instructions on getting your gold assayed and sold:

http://www.ehow.com/how_2324121_sell-gold-dust.html

http://www.prescottlab.com/

Once you have your gold assayed, you have an idea what it is worth. You should find out what the percentage of gold is in the dust you have collected. You should find this out from the assay results.

Next, you will look for a good place to sell your gold. Find out who are reliable gold buyers and shop around for the best deal. Make sure you check the reputation of the buyer, because once you ship your gold to the buyer, you have to have trust that you will get paid.

Send your shipment with enough insurance to cover the value of your gold dust in the event that it gets lost (it happens frequently in the case of gold.) Here is a link to a website that rates various gold buyers (but you should do your own research.)

http://reviewgoldbuyers.org/?gclid=CL30nKTm_rACFY2b7Qodlkf5ew

I will not go into more detail on this business, but be sure to read the general business requirements in the Appendix.

86. Search for Meteorites

I suppose everyone has seen the show 'Meteorite Men' on TV. If you have, you know that there is money in finding meteorites, if you are good at it. But you must be willing to do research and to travel to where the meteorites can be found in different places in the USA and around the world.

If you don't know anything about meteorites, there is an excellent book that you can obtain. The name of the book is *"Rocks from Space"* by O. Richard Norton. Here is a link where you can buy the book online:

http://www.amazon.com/Rocks-Space-Meteorites-Meteorite-Astronomy/dp/0878423737/ref=sr_1_1?s=books&ie=UTF8&qid=1341524148&sr=1-1&keywords=Rocks+from+Space

Here is a link to a site that has a lot of good information about meteorites and what their values are, approximately, for different kinds:

http://geology.com/meteorites/value-of-meteorites.shtml

So where can you find meteorites? There are a number of places around the world where meteors have impacted on the earth. The places where meteors have landed are generally called 'meteorite strewnfields' because the meteors usually land at an angle to the earth's surface and break up leaving an area behind them where you can find pieces of the meteorites. This area is called the 'strewnfield'.

So where exactly are these strewnfields located? When a meteorite hunter finds a strewnfield where he finds good pieces of meteorites, he usually keeps his find secret so that others cannot come and pick the area. So some fields are secret, but some are also publically known.

The publically known areas are usually well picked, unless they are in very remote and hard to access places. Here are some links to sites that will help you find locations of meteorite strewnfields:

http://en.wikipedia.org/wiki/Meteorite#The_Great_Plains_of_the_US

http://www.lpi.usra.edu/science/kring/epo_web/arizona_meteorites/

http://www.lpi.usra.edu/meteor/index.php

Using the last of the above 3 sites, I ran a search on 'all countries' and then did a search on South America with the following results:

http://www.passc.net/EarthImpactDatabase/SouthAmerica.html

So what kind of equipment do you need? Iron bearing meteorites are fairly easily detected with a good metal detector and a stick with a strong magnet on the end of it. You can make your own magnetic stick for surface hunting.

 I made one with an aluminum tube and a bar magnet attached to one end. I bent the other end of the tube to form a convenient handle for holding the stick while walking. Here is an example of a stick that folds up when you don't need it, but it can be extended to test a rock:

http://www.amazon.com/SE-15Lb-Magnet-Pick-up-Tool/dp/B000RB3XBA/ref=sr_1_40?ie=UTF8&qid=1341606573&sr=8-40&keywords=magnets

 The metal detector will find iron-nickel meteorites that are buried, but not too deep, depending on the depth that the detector will sense down to. Generally, the better the detector, the deeper down it will detect meteorites.

When you are starting out, do not spend too much money on a metal detector until you see if you really want to search for meteorites, as you must have a lot of patience, and your search will usually be under extreme conditions of hot or cold. You may search all day and not find a thing. Other days you might be lucky and hit the jackpot. Like most businesses, you will have to work hard and have a lot of patience.

So where can you sell your meteorites? If you find a really big one, you might be able to sell it to a Museum. Be sure to document all of your finds because collectors want to know where it was found and whatever pertinent information you have on it (but keep the exact location secret, unless you are not going to search at that place again.)

Meteorites that have hit something like a house, a car, a barn, or other man-made structures are especially valuable provided you are able to document where they were found and have corroboration from witnesses that might have seen the event. Photographs of the damage are very helpful.

A few things to be aware of:

(1) Any meteorites found on US Government land are automatically owned by the Smithsonian Institute and it is against federal law to remove or take them.

(2) In Canada, you must get an export license from the government before you can take a meteorite out of the country.

3) If you want to hunt on private land anywhere (in USA, for example), you must get permission from the owner of the land, otherwise you may be charged with trespassing and theft of property.

If you are just starting out, hunt at locations until you find out if meteorite hunting is really for you, instead of spending a lot of money traveling to some remote location. Also, be sure you know what kind of meteorites you are looking for. There are a number of different types such as Iron-nickel, carbonaceous, etc.

I will not go into more detail on this business, but be sure to read the general business requirements in the Appendix.

87. Start a Guard Business

If you are an ex-serviceman, an ex-policeman, or you are a weapons expert familiar with defensive and offensive tactics using a weapon or martial arts, you may be interested in starting a guard service.

Who needs a guard service? Many business places and even some personal residences use a guard service. Also, plants or businesses that do military contracting usually have a guard at the gates, or in the front office to screen visitors, etc. Most guard jobs require a hand gun to be in the possession of the guard, and carried in a visible manner.

Dance clubs and other night spots also higher so-called "bouncers" to get rid of 'tough customers', but usually no uniform is worn by the bouncers and they do not carry weapons, at least that are visible. So there is plenty of business to be obtained, especially in the larger cities.

This business does not require a lot of capital to get started. It does require that you are knowledgeable and can train your guards in what they need to know to be effective guards.

Remember that your guards represent you and they will be the prime source of people's impression of you and your business. Are your guards friendly? Are they polite? Do they greet people that come into the establishment every day that they know (especially the executives and the boss?) Are they helpful? Another thing to include in your training is for the guards to apply minimum force when force is required to control an unruly or 'tough customer'.

A guard should not ever strike a person. That could lead to an assault and battery charge. The guard should use wrestling holds or martial arts techniques that can control a person without striking with the hand or fist. A good way to control a violent person is to try to get a head-lock on him from behind.

It is very difficult to break such a hold if properly applied. The subject can then be marched out of the establishment, or wrestled to floor and held there until help can be summoned. If there is not other method of controlling someone, the guard may have to draw his weapon, but this should be a last resort.

Of course, if the subject has a weapon and has already drawn it on the guard, the guard should not draw his weapon as it would be a death warrant for him to do so. By the way, the guard have an electronic button on his belt that he can easily push which will summon help to his location (such a device is often carried by elderly people to summon help in the case that they would fall or have some kind of an attack.) ADT has a service like this that you can subscribe to and have your guards connected.

The more professional your guards are on the job, the more likely you are to retain the account. Your guards should have good looking uniforms and good quality tools, such as radios, flashlights, a night stick, and quality hand guns.

A guard should be able to call you on a radio quickly for advice in difficult situations, or to alert you of trouble. Their hand gun should be at least a 9mm or a 0.45 caliber weapon. A .38 standard police issue revolver would also be acceptable. Here is an example of a site where you can buy firearms online:

http://www.ableammo.com/catalog/default.php?cPath=9935

Make sure your guards are properly licensed to carry their weapon and are well trained in its use. Periodic target practice and fast-draw techniques should be mandatory to retain their job. Here is an example of a website where you can order uniforms for your guards.

http://www.automotiveworkwear.com/mm5/merchant.mvc?Store_Code=AW&Screen=CTGY&Category_Code=Security-Uniforms&Offset=0

Here is an example of a site where you can order security guard accessories:

It is also good to train your guards in hand-to-
hand combat in case they cannot draw their
weapon in time to defend themselves. Your
guards do not have to be young but they do need
to be fit and it would be a good idea to test their
fitness periodically.

A good fitness test is for a guard to be able to jog
or run a one mile course without stopping to rest.
It would be best if you could do this yourself also
so you can lead their periodic fitness run.

Strength training (lifting weights, etc.) is also a
good idea.

One way to get your business started is to get one
man (or a woman) under contract to act as a
guard for you, and then start marketing your
services to companies. Once you have one guard
placed in a job, then you can contract another
guard for the next account you obtain. So you
contract and place one guard at a time to build up
your business. If you contract capable and
profession people, you should do well in this
business.

But how can you market your business? First tell
all of your friends and acquaintances that you are
starting a security guard business. You may place
small advertisements in the newspaper and send
flyers to various businesses that you think may be
potential customers. You should join business

oriented service clubs, such as the Rotary club, where you can meet business people and develop your business contacts.

Get business cards printed that you can hand to contacts. Create a website where you describe your business and list the services that you provide. Provide a way for the public to contact you, but be careful that you do not reveal your name or the location of your home. Do not use your home phone number as it can easily used to find out where you live. It you have a brick and mortar office somewhere, make it look inconspicuous and do not put your business name on the outside of the building.

Your guards, of course, will know where your office is located. It's a good idea to eventually have a building and some grounds that you can use for training and target practice for your guards, but you do not need it to get the business started. It you do get a building somewhere, it should be in a rural location where you will not disturb neighbors. I will not go into more detail on this business, but be sure to read the general business requirements in the Appendix.

88. Become a Real Estate Agent

Being a real estate agent is not exactly having your own business, but you are in many ways your own boss, and it is up to you whether you are successful or not. If you become a real estate broker, then you can start your own business.

To become a real estate agent you would normally need to take a short course so that you can pass the real estate agent test in your local area or state. Most areas require a real estate agent to be licensed, and you have to renew your license periodically.

After you pass your test you will most likely have to pay a fee to become a registered agent with a broker so that you can use the services of the local real estate association. The services may include what is commonly referred to as the Multiple Listing Service. This service is usually a computer website that you can access (if you are registered.)

The site allows you to scan through the properties that are listed for sale by the service. You will need that to be able to find properties that fit the needs of your customers and show the properties to them.

There are a few things you will need in this career. First of all you will need a very high level of patience because people are very cautious about buying property and the least little problem or defect with the property will usually cause them to drop the property from any further consideration.

You will have to have patience with every customer in order to make a sale. You may have to show a customer a dozen or more properties before you make a sale, or maybe you never make a sale with the customer. You will need a large vehicle like a SUV or a van to haul your customers to the property you show them.

You will have to invest in a considerable amount of gasoline in the process, so try to make your trips count. Don't waste time with people that you know do not have the money to buy properties, are just curious, or out to get chauffeured around town. Women agents should be cautious about meeting customers that they do not know. It is good practice to bring someone with you the first time you meet a customer.

The next thing you need is good support from the broker you are working with. When you are first starting out, and even after you have experience, it is best to work under a lead agent that may have several people in his group.

You will find out that the paperwork and laws covering real estate transactions are very complicated and you have to be able to write up real estate contracts for sale of a property yourself. You cannot ask another agent or the broker to do it for you.

Of course, you may need some help to get started doing contracts. One thing you should know is that sophisticated customers may want to add all kinds of weird conditions on their offers to the seller. You must oblige, no matter how silly, unless you know a certain requirement is already covered by state real estate law, is covered in the standard contract form, or the requirement the customer wants is against the law.

Your group leader, or an assigned agent, if not the broker, will provide you with support and training that the head broker does not have time to give you, because he or she may have a large number of agents working for him or her. You need to market yourself to friends and acquaintances.

Make sure that they know that you are available to help them with their real estate questions. Be willing to help them with any questions they may have, even if you know they probably will not sell their existing home, or ever buy a new or different home. You should also join service clubs such as the Rotary and Kiwanis clubs. Be sure to help with the club projects and do a good job so that you will be a respected member.

Get business cards printed that you can hand out to your contacts. Note that you could also work for a home builder on the side to have the chance to sell the properties he has built or will build to suit the customer. There are several areas you can specialize in. Most agents concentrate on home sales work.

But you could also specialize in commercial properties, apartment buildings, unimproved land, or a combination of properties. Whatever specialties(s) you decide to work with, you must be knowledgeable in it, if not expert. The more you know about the properties you are selling, the more you will impress your customers. This is not a business that you can do part-time. You must be totally dedicated, and work very hard, to be successful in this business.

Most states will allow you to apply for a broker's license and take the test after you have gained one or two years experience working for a broker. Note that it is difficult to start a new real estate brokerage, so you may just want to continue being just an agent. You can still work for your broker's license, and there are additional real estate education goals and certifications you can work for.

One additional advantage of being a real estate agent is that you learn about bargain properties for sale in your area. You might start a business on the side where you buy a bargain property and then get it cleaned up and re-modeled for resale. You may be part of a group that does this work so that you have help getting the properties remodeled.

I will not go into more detail on this career, but be sure to read the general business requirements in the Appendix.

89. Become a Physical Trainer

If you are a healthy and fit person with an understanding of exercise equipment and strength training, you may be interested in becoming a physical trainer. How does it work? First you have to get certified as a trainer.

The requirements vary from state-to-state. You will have to probably take some course work and

take a test to get your certification. Here is the website for a certification organization (I show this as an example only.
You should do your own research to find the best certification organization and educational programs in your area, or online educational programs.)

http://www.ncsf.org/

So how much can you make being a physical trainer? An average charge for professional training is $35 for a 30 minute session. Where can you find work as a personal trainer? Any gym that serves the public with exercise equipment such as treadmills, weight machines, and free weights as well as other equipment, is a possible place for you to do business.
Some gyms employee trainers to serve their members. In this case you are an employee. You can also be a freelance trainer, where you do not work for a gym but work directly with your own customers from whom you get paid directly.
Most gyms will allow you to come in and train someone in their gym if you have previously made arrangements with the gym to use their facilities. You may have to become a member of that gym and pay a fee to train people there. You would pass these costs on to your customers as part of your hourly rate.
The same gyms will usually allow you to post your information, picture, certification

information, and your contact information on their walls or bulletin boards so that members of the gym will know about the services you provide. Also, as a freelance trainer, you can advertise in your local newspaper and have your own website to advertise your services.

Your major investment to work in this profession will be getting the education required to gain certification. You will need to know a good bit of anatomy, especially the muscular and skeletal parts of human anatomy. You will also have to be familiar with the operation and settings of the large array of different exercise equipment, that are of professional quality that you find in the better equipped gyms. To get started in this business, tell all of your friends and acquaintances that you have become a certified physical trainer (wait until you are certified before you start marketing your services.)

Make arrangements with several quality gyms to be allowed to train people in their gym. To get started working at the gyms you need to 'prime the pump'. One way to do this is to find a friend or someone who would like to train with you free of charge or at a very low cost for a period of time. Pay for his or her gym memberships and meet at the various gyms with him or her for training sessions.

Why should you do this? It is a way to become visible to other gym members and a way to encourage people to ask you to train them. You will find that you have competition for customers so you need to keep your rates competitive. You will also find that some trainers have more than one certification to their credit, or they have a higher certification than you do, but don't be discouraged and keep advancing your physical training knowledge.

Apply for more or higher levels of certification when you are ready to do so. You will find that training people will be a rewarding experience for you when you see the people become stronger, more physically fit, and develop more confidence in themselves. I will not go into more detail on this business, but be sure to read the general business requirements in the Appendix.

90. Trade Goods

If you have a lot of goods or "stuff" that you don't really need, but there are items that you need or want but don't have, you may be interested in trading what you have for something else. This can be done online by joining a trading or bartering group online and swapping what you have for what someone else has.

I suppose everyone has heard stories of people trading a small item, such as a camera, for something better, and then trading the new item for something better yet, until he or she ends up owning something valuable such as a car for example. That is probably a difficult feat to perform but maybe not impossible for a sharp trader who knows the value of goods of various kinds.

A really good trader might even be able to create a business out of the process. Since no money changes hands, there is no income to report on your income tax, so this is a big advantage of trading. Of course if you sell the goods you have obtained by trading as a business, then you have income to report. Here is a site that does a good job of how trading online works:

http://www.swaptreasures.com/blog/?p=11

Here is the trading site that is referenced by the above link and is an example of one trading site a person can join (but do your own research to find sites that fit your needs),

http://www.swaptreasures.com/

As an alternative, you could place advertisements in your local newspaper for items that you want to trade, but you will have to pay for ads, whereas there is no cost to list your item on a free trading website. A good trading site will not charge you to join their site. It is merely a vehicle to put you in touch with members that want items or have items that you might want to swap for. The whole process is based on trust so you have to have a little courage to ship something to someone and believe that you will receive something back. Start with small, not very expensive items, and try to build up a network of trading partners that you have had good luck with and that you have developed trust with.

As you gain experience and have developed a trusted network of trading partners, then you can start trading more valuable items that you want to trade. You will list the items you have that you want to trade and you can see the lists of items that other people have to trade on the site you decide to work with. Make sure you like the way the site works that you have decided to use.

The larger the numbers they have listed as members, the better your trading experience should be, so be sure you know how big the group is that the site works with. You may become members on several sites to increase the size of your trading group. You should develop one network at a time however, so that you do not get spread too thin, and keep jumping from one site to another which is wasting your time.

So what kind of items can be traded? Almost anything, like tools, cars, boats, antiques, books, CDs, DVDs, cameras, hundreds if not thousands of other items. But don't waste your time and someone else's time trying to trade items that are worn-out, broken, dirty, or with some major defect that makes the item worthwhile.

Also if you trade a defective item to someone who is expecting something better from you, it will be a black mark on your reputation. The recipient of your item may even report you for abuse and damage your reputation for the whole group.

So be sure your trading partner is well informed on the condition of the item you are sending to him or her. In fact it is always good policy to understate the quality of the item so your trading partner will be pleasantly surprised. For example, suppose you have a popular movie DVD that is mint in every way including the package, you could describe the item as "good", instead of saying "mint" or "new".

When your trading partner receives the item he or she should be satisfied or even impressed with the quality of the item you have traded to him. So how could you make a business out of trading? One way would be to trade a valuable or expensive item for a collection of items of lesser value.

Eventually you may have enough "stuff" to open a store, either a 'brick and mortar' store, or an online operation. You could use E-bay to auction your items for cash, or set up your own website store.

I will not go into more detail on this activity, but if you are going to make it a business, be sure to read the general business requirements in the Appendix.

91. Be a Wilderness Guide

If you are very familiar with a certain wilderness area, enough so that you could lead people to the best fishing spots, or the best hunting spots, and you are expert in the arts of hunting, fishing, canoeing, camping, you can be a guide who leads groups or individual in the area.

Or if you are familiar with a certain ocean (or Great Lakes region) fishing area and you are capable of operating a sport deep sea fishing vessel and handling deep sea fishing rigs, you could be a professional fisherman, taking individuals or small groups to good fishing areas. Is there enough money to make a living in this business?

Yes, if you are good at guiding and can build up a steady business. How much should you charge for your services? It depends on the area you are working in, and how much your competition is charging.

It will also depend on how dangerous your guide area is, for example is it deep in the Amazon jungle, in an African country where there are animals dangerous to humans? So how would you advertise your business? The best way is to run small ads in the classified section of magazines such as *Sports Afield, Field and Stream, Sports Illustrated, Adventure World Magazine, Women's Adventure Magazine, National Geographic Adventure* (magazine) and other sporting magazines.

There are also a lot of online classified sites where you can place your advertisement for free. Here is one example:

What licenses do you need? Usually you will need fishing and hunting licenses. You may also need a guide license, if it is required in your state or area you work in. Are there any professional guide associations? Yes, for some areas. For example the US state of Maine has a guide association. Here is their website:

http://www.maineguides.org/guidesallguides.php

To be a good guide, you need to be friendly and helpful to your customers, but you also have to command respect and maintain discipline in the group you are guiding. Don't ever let someone go off by themselves, or "go off the reservation". If you are guiding a large group, you must be especially watchful of the people in your group. One good thing to do is to use the "buddy system".

The way it works is to pair up people who you assign to stay together throughout the trip. Each person in the pair is responsible for the safety and well being of the other. A couple of things to watch out for is people who get a bad blister on a foot, or who get their feet wet and don't remove their boots at night to let their feet and boots dry for the next day. It is a good idea to tell the people that you will guide, how to dress and equip themselves for the trip.

Such things as waterproof boots and insulated boots for cold weather, insect repellant, water proofed tents, sleeping bags, a good back pack for extended trips, etc. Also, you should have a set of safety rules to be followed during the trip. For example, don't wear cotton clothes in winter trips (cotton is the "death fabric" because it will absorb and hold 30 times its weight of water), firearms must be carried in an unloaded state until you direct otherwise, a list of clothing and footwear that you approve of for the trip, limits on campfires and how to put them out before leaving the camping area, life jackets must be worn during water sports, what to do during emergencies, and so forth.

Always obey the rules of the Forrest Service and any instructions you might get from Game Wardens, or other law enforcement officials, and make sure everyone in your group follows the rules. You will know if you are suited to the guide business or not.

I will not go into more detail on this business, but be sure to read the general business requirements in the Appendix.

92. Become a Travel Guide

How would you like to travel to Europe, Asia, New Zealand, or Australia and make money by doing so? Most people would jump at a chance like that. But to do so means that you will have to invest a little money and time to learn to be a travel guide for the areas you want to visit.

What do you need to do to be a travel guide? The first thing to do is to start with one area, for example you might start with a country that you know the language in common usage in that country. Maybe you know Italian. Then you would probably be able to travel to Italy and in doing so learn all of the problems and solutions involved in getting there with as little hassle as possible and being able to visit the major tourist attractions in a reasonable amount of time.

You should also find reasonable accommodations that are clean but not over-priced. You would probably make notes on the best places to visit, when to visit them, and the best means of transportation to get to them. You might have to make more than one trip to each area to "learn the ropes" before you arrange to take groups there.

One thing to try to do is to make arrangements with businesses such as restaurants, and hotels, to get discounts if you bring your group there (always make sure you call ahead to make proper reservations.) You may also become allied with expert local guides that will sub-contract to you to handle some or all of the guiding of your group once you have taken your group to the area he is expert in.

Such expert local guides would also be a help to you in learning the area if you went with them once or twice yourself. Once you have learned an area well, you are in a position to start organizing tours with groups. Make sure you have all the bases covered such as required visas, travel permits, money conversion, travel and transportation tickets, reservations, and accommodations, and a host of other items to deal with.

How could you market your services? One thing to do is get to know travel agents around your local area and around the country you are going to lead tours from. Arrange to give an agent a commission if he or she helps you get a group lined up for a tour. You will need to get some brochures and business cards printed that you can pass out.

Also you could place small advertisements in travel magazines. Here are some magazines that you might place ads in: *Adventure World Magazine, Women's Adventure Magazine, National Geographic Adventure* (magazine), *Caribbean Travel + Life, National Geographic Traveler (magazine), Travel + More, Budget Travel*, and others.

Your main assets in this business are your knowledge of travel techniques and places to visit, your ability to deal with individuals and groups, your friendliness, and your ability to make friends and communicate with people. You will know if this business if for you or not.

I will not go into more details on this business, but be sure to read the general business requirements in the Appendix.

93. Become an Investment Advisor

Why should you become an investment advisor?
Because you can be an independent business man
and you can make a good living if you are good
at it. Also you can help people save and invest
their money more wisely possibly protecting
them from large financial loses making rash and
uninformed investments.
So if you do your job well and ethically, you
should get a certain amount of satisfaction from
this work. I don't recommend this business for
everybody. You should have at least some
financial or business education, investment
experience, and have a good knowledge of the
various markets, such as the stock market,
futures, options, commodities, metals (gold,
copper, silver, etc.), currency speculation, mutual
funds, exchange traded funds, bonds, and so
forth.
Obviously, some investments are more risky than
others. Different people have different tolerances
for risk. For example, a young working person
should have a higher proportion of stocks, or
stock funds, than Treasury bonds, certificates of
deposit, or cash, than an older person getting
ready for retirement, or already retired. Another
common problem is that one person needs to
withdraw more cash or income from their
investment account than others.

Each person in theory should have his or her asset allocation calculated for their age, income, total net worth, tolerance for risk, and other factors. So what do you have to do to become a registered investment advisor.

The requirements vary from state to state, but usually involves mainly a filing fee, various forms to fill out, a statement of capital assets, a minimum amount of capital in your business, and a surety bond, especially if you are a custodian of customer funds, or if you have discretionary power over customer accounts.

You will also have to be familiar with SEC security law and be able to pass a test to get your securities license for the state you operate in. That license allows you to sell securities to a customer, or trade securities for your customer.

It would also be a good idea to get an insurance agent's license so you are allowed to sell life insurance or other types of insurance to your customers. You will have to be knowledgeable in various kinds of insurance and pass a test to get your insurance agents license. You could also have an insurance agency set up to be another business you run along with being an investment advisor.

In the advisor business, you have the possibility of forming a securities investment firm once you have accumulated enough capital. For example, once you have $1,000,000 in capital you could form a fund know as a "hedge fund" in the

United States. So how would you set-up your business?

First of all, to look professional, you will need a brick and mortar location. It should be in a good neighborhood where there is good traffic. A good location would be a store front in an up-scale shopping center, or a building that has other reputable business offices. Be sure to tell all your friends and acquaintances that you are going to be an investment advisor. Get some business cards printed that you can pass out.

Put small advertisements in business magazines and newspapers. Join some service clubs such as the Rotary and Kiwanis and be active in the clubs so people will get to know and trust you. Get a good website set up that tells what you do and has your contact information. I will not go into more detail on the investment advisor business, but be sure to read the general business requirements in the Appendix.

94. Start a Pizza Business

Why would anyone start a pizza business with so many existing pizza businesses almost anywhere? My answer is that virtually all of the existing pizza businesses, either eat-in places, or home delivery operations, have more of less the same types of pizza. Another factor is that you can buy 12 inch pizzas in the supermarket that are as good or better than the franchise pizza operations (you know who they are.) So how could you make money in this business?

I think the way you could build a successful pizza business is to create your style and line of pizzas that are different but better in taste (made to order on-site), and have a better selection of crusts and toppings. Finally, you can beat the competition by charging less, and creating unique recipes at better values for your customers.

One advantage you will have is that the franchise stores in your area charge relatively high prices (poor values for what you get) and they are not flexible in changing their prices (because they are limited by their franchise requirements.) So in general you can beat their prices.

So in pricing your product, your only worry is the independent pizza operations your area (which are probably very few) that might try to undercut you on prices. So what are some of the ways you could beat the franchises? First of all, the franchisers have fixed styles with limited ability to be flexible on toppings and types of pizzas.

You could have a system where the customer can specify exactly what type of pizza he wants (cheese, chicken, pepperoni, thick crust, thin crust, etc.) and what kind of mix of toppings, so that in effect the customer can design his own pizza made to order.

You could either do home delivery or eat-in. In either case, you will need a brick and mortar building, and a good pizza oven. If you do an eat-in business, you will have to have more

employees. This would be a good business for a family to operate where everyone who works is a partner in the business and not an employee.
This saves a lot of book-keeping hassle, payroll, tax collection, health insurance, and a lot of other government laws and regulations. If you do a home delivery only business, you should consider using only contract labor for deliveries, and partnerships for your workers that prepare the pizzas for delivery.

The contract delivery people would provide their own vehicles and pay all of their vehicle expenses, including gasoline, oil, and maintenance. You should be the main cook or chef, and the principle owner to keep control of your business.

I will not go into more detail on this business, but be sure to read the general business requirements in the Appendix.

95. Coil Winding

If you have mechanical ability, you have some electrical knowledge, the ability to do some calculations, and the ability to read and understand electrical component specifications, you could wind coils as a part-time business or even a fulltime business. What kinds of coils? There is a variety of coils that electronics companies require, such as radio frequency coils, power inductors, transformers, chokes, electric motor re-winding, and a lot of specialty coils and other electro-magnetic devices. Coils are either wound on a bobbin (like sewing thread), as a toroid, and other physical geometries.

Some coils, usually low frequency coils, have iron or ferrite cores. Other coils have "air core" coils, for example usually radio or high frequency coils. Air core coils do have a problem with "saturation" like iron or ferrite core coils do, so they are sometimes used in high end audio applications.

Coils that are used in mass production applications such as consumer electronic systems (television, etc.) are generally first "prototyped" so that an engineer can test their performance in his circuit design. This is where you come in. You would probably only wind a few or a very limited quantity of "prototypes" that you make to an engineer's specification.

Most likely a lot of the coil winding you will do, will be done by hand with the aid of a manual machine. Eventually, you may invest in automatic equipment to make certain coils in higher volume, but that is not where you should start.

You need to start slowly and learn the business first, if you are not already experienced in this work. Here is a website of a coil winding machine manufacturer that makes both bobbin and toroid winding machines (I don't necessarily recommend this company. You should do your own research.)

http://www.gormanmachine.com/

Here is the website for technical documents from Magnetics Inc. This company is known for its reliability and good service:

http://www.mag-inc.com/design/technical-documents

There are numerous other technical articles and inductor/coil design information on the internet. Here is a link to an excellent design article which has basic information and equations. Do not let the math scare you. It is all basic high school algebra.

http://ecee.colorado.edu/copec/book/slides/Ch14slides.pdf

So how would you promote your business? The best way is to place targeted advertising on Google. The targeting is based on someone's search subject. For example, if someone searches for inductors or coils, your ad would appear in the right-hand side column of advertisements. Another way is to place small ads in various electronics magazines, such as Electronics Magazine, Design Magazine, R & D Magazine, etc.

I will not go into more detail on this business, but be sure to read the general business requirements in the Appendix.

96. Drive an Ice Cream Truck

Driving an ice cream truck is at least a good part-time business if you work hard and are able to buy quality ice cream in bulk at low prices. The best hours for your ice cream business will be from afternoon to early evening.

You will need a panel truck with large ice chests that you can load with ice to keep your ice cream cold as you run your route. In extremely hot weather (your best time to sell ice cream) you may keep your ice cream colder with dry ice, but you do not want the ice cream so cold that you cannot scoop it.

Your truck should be a late model panel truck in good shape. Your truck should have a fresh paint job in gleaming white, or an original white finish that still has a shine. (If your truck is an old "junker" with bad paint, forget using that truck in your business, and get a better truck.) It is a "must" to establish your business name and get it painted in large letters on the sides and back or your truck.

For example "Joe's Super Cold Ice Cream" with your phone number and a website name if you have one. Get an artist to paint some ice cream cones and a picture representing some kind icy cold logo or picture that will remind people of something cold and frosty. You will need a PA system to play music or chimes that children will recognize as your ice cream truck.

Always use the same theme music, whatever it is (and make sure you have a permit to operate a public address system on your truck.) Your image will be everything. Pass out flyers in the neighborhoods you intend to cover. Make sure you get very high quality ice cream, vanilla cones, and cake cones.

Cheap ice cream will not sell well. Be sure to have standard flavors that children can understand, such as vanilla, chocolate, and strawberry. You may also have other flavors that kids might like, but don't go overboard on flavors until you know what kids will buy. You might add one flavor at a time and see how it sells until you have a popular selection.

Keep your ice cream reasonably priced so your prices do not get parents upset. Also be sure to watch out for competition and make sure you are not undersold. Never give children anything with nuts or peanuts on it. Some children are allergic to nuts, and especially peanuts.

A money changer on your belt will allow you to make change faster. Make sure that you keep everything clean, especially your hands, and your truck inside and out. Parents will check you out by looking at your truck and your appearance. Wear a clean white shirt and white pants. White shoes would also look good. It would be a plus if your shirts had your logo embroidered on them.

Make sure you use food handling papers or paper covered cones when serving customers and changing money. The best neighborhoods will be in areas where a lot of young couples have children. Don't waste your time in neighborhoods where there are few if any children.

Always be nice to the children that come to your truck and try to give them what they want. Never act grumpy or like you are doing them a favor selling them ice cream. Try to make friends with as many children as possible, always treating them with respect.

Kids like a friendly, outgoing personality. Call yourself "Uncle Joe" or some other friendly name. Below are some website links for companies that supply wholesale ice cream (but be careful to do your own research before you commit to any one company.)

http://www.chocolateshoppeicecream.com/wholesaleicecream

http://www.berlinerfoods.com/

http://www.omhicecream.com/index.php

http://ny-icecream.com/Home_Page.html

The business has possibilities for expansion. One way would be to acquire additional trucks and contract people to operate them for you on a contract basis. This business is popular with college students that want to make money during the summer months.

I will not go into more detail on this business, but be sure to read the general business requirements in the Appendix.

97. Make Skin Cream

Did you ever think about making skin lotion? Why would you do that? Because most of the skin lotions (body lotions, face creams, etc.) are made from synthetic chemicals that could be absorbed through a person's skin and possibly cause a health problem, at least that is what a lot of people think.

What does this fact result in? The dislike of synthetic chemical lotions, produces a market for organic "pure" lotions that are often marketed at high prices. Is there any real reason to use skin lotions anyway? Probably not for young healthy people, but older people tend to have problems with dry skin that can cause roughness or even cracking of the skin, resulting in painful and sometimes deep sores.

Also men who do labor work in cold weather under low humidity conditions often get very dry hands and cracks in the skin, also with possible sores. So, how could you make skin lotions for sale? There is lots of good information on recipes, and methods of making lotions. The first link below seems to have the best information.

One thing to be aware of is that most recipes have beeswax as an ingredient.

There are people who are allergic to beeswax, so I don't recommend the use of beeswax as an emulsifying agent. You can buy emulsifying wax instead to use in your recipe (This is described in the first link below.) You should only use an emulsifying agent that is approved for use in food products. That way you will be certain it is safe for use as a skin lotion. Note that once you incorporate the commercial emulsifying agent, your formula is not strictly organic anymore, so you may have to give your cream a different name, such as "Nature's Healing Lotion", or whatever, as long as you don't claim it is totally "organic".

There are other emulsifying agents that are used in food, some of which could be "organic" such as lecithin, eggs, milk, mustard, gelatin, and others. A strong emulsifying agent used in bread making is diacetyl tartaric esters of monoglycerides. See the next to the last link in the link list below.

So how could you get this business started?

There are probably many ways, but I suggest that you first work out your formula until you get a good consistency and a lotion that has a pleasant feeling on your skin.

You may add some fragrance to your formula to give it a pleasing aroma (But be careful. Is the fragrance safe? Is it "organic", or is it a synthetic chemical?) If you have a fragrant lotion, you should also have an unscented version, because a lot of people do not like scented lotions.

You should also add a preservative to your formula to have a long shelf life. The following link will lead you to an organic preservative called "BIOSECUR" ™.

This preservative is specifically made for things like cosmetics including personal care items such as skin lotions (but be sure to do your own research and testing on anything you add to your formula that you are not totally confident of.)

http://www.biosecur.com/biosecur/personal-care-preservatives/personal-care-preservatives-united-states/

Do not add a coloring agent. If you do it might not meet FDA requirements (see FDA requirements, the last link in the link list below.) By the way, make sure you do not add any poisonous ingredient to your formula and make sure your label clearly shows all ingredients you have in your formula.

This is an FDA requirement. You should consult a food chemist to make sure all of your ingredients are safe. Also make sure you label includes warnings such as "for external use only" and "not for ophthalmic use", or "do not apply in or near eyes."

Note also that the FDA can inspect your manufacturing facility at any time, and that you are responsible for the sanitary and safe manufacturing of your product, even if you have contracted your product out to be manufactured in an off-shore plant.

If you do not live in the USA, be sure to find out what government requirements are applicable in your area. However, if you expect to import your product into the USA, you will still have to meet FDA requirements to get it through US Customs. You can do the experimental work in your kitchen or garage. Once you have your formula worked out, you should find some volunteers to try your lotion, and have them fill out an evaluation questionnaire after they have used the lotion. Ask them to give you a testimonial on their evaluation (if they like it.)

You may have to pay some money to your volunteers to do this work for you. Of course you will give your volunteers free samples of your product also. If you get your family and friends to help you with the evaluation, it may not cost you anything except the materials and time you put in making the lotion samples.

Once you have your evaluations completed you should do an honest analysis of the results. Is your product good enough to market or not? Do you have something worthwhile to sell that you could market to people with enthusiasm and sincerity, and that would really be helpful to them? If so you may be ready for the next step. Otherwise go back and re-do your formula to make it better, until you get it right.

If you are ready, you should make all necessary arrangements to be ready for production. Select the jars or containers you plan to use and have your sources for all your materials lined up. Order sample quantities of all of your materials including containers (this is a step of faith it will be a small investment, so be sure you are ready to start.)

Make sure all of your suppliers are trustworthy and reliable. Make arrangements to have someone, or some contract manufacturing company, ready to make your product in small quantities to start with (or make samples yourself to start with.) Get artwork done on a nice label for your containers and select a printer to print and cut a small stock ready to use. They should be done on paper with a sticky backing for easy application to your containers. Is the next step to manufacturer your product in quantity?

No, your next step is to start marketing your product. Do not go into production until you start getting significant orders and feel confident enough to start building a small inventory to ship from. Caution, do not order too much at any one time.

Don't let your inventory get to large compared to your sales. So how will you market your product? First of all make sure you have all of your business requirements done to operate your business (see the Appendix.) Your product falls into the general category of "cosmetics" so you will have to meet all government requirements for selling cosmetics in your area, but a cosmetic does not need the FDA pre-approval like drugs and foods do. You will need to have a website set up as a "store".

You can recruit distributors. Despite what people say about "pyramid" schemes, it is a valid marketing technique. Lots of companies have used the pyramid marketing structure for years successfully. You have probably heard of Amway, for one.

Good avenues to advertise in are online services such as Facebook, Google, and Twitter, as well as others. Both Facebook and Twitter allow advertising without cost in- stream.

I estimate that 40 to 50% of the "tweets" on Twitter are marketing of one sort or another for some kind of business, including cosmetics. If you can get your products "hawked" on television venues such as the Home Shopping Network, you have a possibility of doing a good business.

I will not go into more details on this business but be sure to follow the general business requirements in the Appendix.

Link List for Business No. 97:

http://asonomagarden.wordpress.com/2009/02/26/how-to-make-handmade-handlotion-w-label-download/

http://www.starwest-botanicals.com/blog/how-to-make-organic-body-lotion.html

http://www.mnn.com/lifestyle/natural-beauty-fashion/stories/make-your-own-natural-body-lotion#

http://www.mnn.com/lifestyle/natural-beauty-fashion/stories/make-your-own-natural-body-lotion#

http://www.biosecur.com/biosecur/personal-care-preservatives/personal-care-preservatives-united-states/

http://www.ehow.com/about_6171416_use-emulsifying-agents-food.html

http://www.fda.gov/Cosmetics/GuidanceCompliance RegulatoryInformation/ucm074162.htm

98. Document Shredding

Have you seen document shredding trucks in your town? Do you live in an area where there are a lot of lawyers, aerospace and/or military contractors? If you do, and you don't see more than one mobile document shredding service in your area, you might consider starting a document shredding service. It is a simple business.

Basically, you have a large van with heavy duty document shredding equipment installed in the back of the truck. You will go to a customer, pick up his documents, and get a guard or other representative of the customer to witness that you shred all of the documents as soon as you move them out of his premises to you truck. That way there is a witness that you did shred the customer's documents which protects both you and your customer. You would also collect documents that the customer has already shredded. You will be paid for your services according to the contract you work out with the customer. You must have a reasonable price structure related to the quantity of documents to be shredded.

Otherwise the customer will find someone else to do the work, or he will do it himself. One way to establish the cost for each visit, is to weigh the documents on a scale before shredding, and then charge a rate of say $0.20 per pound (for example), so if a pickup is 100 pounds, you would charge the customer $20.

You could have a rate set so that the more the customer has to shred, the cheaper his rate becomes. The secret will be to have a lot of customers and a good route established so that you don't waste gasoline driving back and forth. Set up a schedule for your customers so they know when to expect you to come to their facility, and this will allow you to establish the shortest route to service all of your customers.

One good feature to have on the back of your truck is a lift-gate, so that all you have to do is pick up the load(s) with a dolly and place it on the lift gate. This prevents the need to lift heavy boxes of documents. Be sure to collect all of the shredded paper and pack it up so you can sell the paper periodically to a paper recycler.

This is a little extra bonus for your business. You will need to market yourself and your business. You should have references, ID, driver's license, truck registration and proof of insurance, and any certifications, liability insurance documents, etc. to show your customer, as required. Be sure to have a good website, and advertise your business in your local newspaper and the "*Yellow Pages*." Your truck does not have to be a new one, but make sure it looks nice and clean. Have your business name and telephone number, etc. painted on the sides and back of your truck. I will not go into more detail on this business, but be sure to read the general business requirements in the Appendix.

99. Build a Shooting Range

If you are a gun owner and live in an urban, or a suburban area, you may have experienced trouble finding a legal place to practice shooting your gun. You may have to drive a long distance to find a legal shooting range.

So if this condition is the case in your area, you may have an opportunity to develop a legal shooting range, depending on local laws and restrictions in your area. To set up a shooting range, you will need to have a location either in a rural location where restrictions do not prevent it, or if you want to set up your business in an urban or suburban area, you will need to have a building in a an area zoned for business and you will have to get permission from your local zoning board.

Some communities have local ordinances with restrictions on gun ranges. Of course you will have to conform to all laws and provide a safe location and a safe set-up. You don't have to have a fancy building. An old building with a large basement is a good possibility if you can do a little interior work to build your shooting range in the building.

A full basement with a large empty area could be set up with partitions to make separate shooting bays, so that one shooter has his own target and does not interfere with the shooters in other bays. In the front of each bay you would have a bench positioned across the bay set a little above average waist height so that a shooter can rest his weapon on the bench, but he cannot enter the bay itself.

His target would be mounted on a string or wire on a continuous loop pulley system so that he can pull his target close to himself to inspect his grouping of shots and mount a new target, pulling the string again to put his target back in the position he wants for firing. The bay should be well lighted and the sides should be marked with distances along the bay so the shooter can put it at any position he wants it at in the bay. You do not have to invest a lot of money making the place look fancy, so your investment should be minimal, except for the rental of the building space you will use. BE SURE to have rules posted for the shooters as to what they can do and cannot do so there is no question what your rules are, and what the local regulations are. It would also be a good idea to have an experienced man to supervise the range and help anyone who is having trouble with their weapon.

The main problem with an indoor range is the need for a way to block bullets at the end of each shooting bay so they do not tear up the back wall of the range. There is a light weight commercially available panel material called "ShotBlocker™" from Norplex-Micarta. The following is a website describing the product:

http://www.shotblocker.com/products.php

Another way is to use mild steel (or AR steel) baffles that are mounted at a about a 30 degree angle facing downward to deflect bullets to a collector. Such baffles need to be at least ¼ inch steel thick (this is the expensive way.) The following website supplies professional baffles for indoor ranges:

Both of the above methods will be expensive and the second will be a lot of work to install. There are other methods using rubber pellets and so forth. The best trap is just plain old dirt or sand placed between panels to hold it in place.
It's a little work to set up. You will have to brace the panels to hold about 1 ½ to 2 feet of dirt. Another method is two walls of concrete blocks back-to-back filled with dirt, and maybe another layer of dirt between the walls. You should put up a large sign on the wall which limits the caliber and loads of bullets to limit damage to your facility. For example as follows:

NO MAGNUM BULLETS OR LOADS.
MAXIMUM HAND GUN CALIBRE 0.45
MAXIMUM RIFLE CALIBRE 0.308
NO BLACK POWDER GUNS OR RIFLES
NO ASSULT WEAPONS
NO MACHINE GUNS

If you are going to build your own shot blocker system, make a small model first and test it with various guns and bullet calibers to see how well it works before you install the full scale version in your range.
There are no doubt other ways to build backstops. Be sure to do your own research. You should also get permission from the building

owner about construction of your shooting bays, backstops and any other construction you might want to do inside his building. Be sure to consult with the owner before you sign a lease or rent the property. Also be sure to check with the local zoning commission.

Another feature you will need in your facility is a good ventilation system that pulls lead fumes away from the shooters and vents to the outside of the building to an alley or other place where there is not much foot traffic. This is a standard health requirement. The ventilation system should be designed so that a slightly negative air pressure is developed inside your facility.

Be sure to add plenty of sound proofing panels inside your shooting bays on walls and ceilings. Carpeting the floors is a good idea for sound reduction and for the foot comfort.

On the first floor, you might have a store where people can rent a legal weapon to shoot, or buy legal weapons from you. Of course you will have to have a Federal Firearms License, and whatever local licenses are required.

If you are going to sell weapons in your business, you will also need a computer to do the required background checks on a customer who wants to buy a legal weapon. Stay away from assault type weapons to avoid trouble. It is best to stick with legal hand guns and hunting rifles, shotguns, and the common ammunitions for legal weapons.

You could also sell gun accessories, hunting clothes, hunting bows and arrows, camping equipment, etc., depending on how big you want your business to be. It is best to start with a minimum investment in inventory, until you know how good your business is going to be (how many people use your facility, and how many people want to buy weapons and other equipment from you.)

Another possibility is to set up a shooting range in a rural area where you have a simple outdoor range and banked dirt barriers at the end of the range to stop bullets. Another way to build a backstop is to lay used truck tires horizontally on top of each other and fill them with sand or dirt. You can probably obtain used truck tires at no cost if you find the right place to ask for them. The following video shows the tire method in an outdoor range:

http://www.youtube.com/watch?v=8gqYiw7PbUY

Also in this case, you have to be careful about shooting rules so that someone does not go out on the range to get their target while someone close by is still shooting downrange. But you can allow more types of legal guns and larger caliber weapons. You will have to supervise people to observe the time divisions between "OK to shoot" and "STOP shooting" for target collection and replacement."

You might have a little shack where people can buy legal ammunition for their guns from you.

You will still have to meet all local regulations and laws. The outdoor range would be a much lower investment than an inside shooting range, but your business options are more limited also. I will not go into more details on this business, but be sure to read the general business requirements in the Appendix.

100. Bow and Arrow Range

A business with a much lower investment and less complex requirements is a bow and arrow range instead of the gun shooting ranges described above. A disadvantage is that there a much lower demand for bow and arrow ranges than gun ranges. If there is more than one range in your area, you should probably go into some other business.

For a bow and arrow range, all you need is a large room with long rectangular dimensions so you can have a reasonable distance to place your targets from the arrow shooting line. Usually people use the large bulls-eye targets packed with straw on a stand. For blocking stray arrows all you need is two layers of ¾ inch plywood panels back-to-back at the end of the range. Make room for a small store section in your range where you can sell bows, arrows, and accessories.

What is the best way to build business in your range? Be sure to join bow and arrow clubs and associations in your area. Become familiar with the sport of bow hunting and the equipment that is used. Arrange bow and arrow contests regularly in your area. You will only be able to do this if you are active in your local bow and arrow clubs and associations.

Especially good are bow hunting clubs because the bow hunters are probably the largest group of bow and arrow shooters in your area, depending on where you live. Wilderness areas are the best place to find bow hunter activity.

If you have some land, you can set up an inexpensive outdoor range with a hunting style course using dear and turkey targets. To get people to come to your outdoor range, do the club and association circuit as I described above.

I will not go into more detail on this business, but be sure to read the general business requirements in the appendix.

101. Sell, Service, and Repair Bicycles

If you have mechanical aptitude and a familiarity with bicycling, you may consider starting a bicycle shop. Bicycling is a hot sport in a lot of areas. But you may have to live in a big city to do a significant business.

Don't sell the cheap stuff that you can buy at the large retail stores. You could fix the cheap ones if someone comes in with one, but your main business should be in high-end and racing type bicycles.

You will be doing more delicate and rewarding work by specializing in the high-end bikes. So how would you get your business going? Be sure to advertise in your local newspapers. The main way to get business though will be to bicycle yourself, on a professional bike, and join a local bicycle club.

Get business cards printed and pass them out at your club when you meet people, but don't be too pushy. All you need for a building is a small store-front shop on a street in a good business area with good traffic.

It would also be good to have a website for your business. Start slow with this business. Don't order a lot of inventory until you see how well you are doing selling bikes. One way to do more business is to offer to obtain bikes for people if you don't have what they want in your store. Find a good source for high quality and professional bikes.

Some bikes are made to order to a special design using special high-strength light weight alloys. This might be a business way to go if you get your original business well established.

Be ready to take care of customers with sources you have researched ahead of time. Be sure to have a selection of popular bicycle accessories available in your store also to sell. After your business gets going good, you should consider contracting a man to handle bike repairs. Make sure the person is qualified and does good work. You cannot tolerate even one mistake in this business because you can be sure all of the bikers in your area will hear about it. I will not go into more details on this business, but be sure to read the general business requirements in the Appendix.

APPENDIX: GENERAL BUSINESS REQUIREMENTS

Here are some general things to consider before you start a business.

1. **Make sure you know what you want to do.** What is your product or service going to be? Don't pick something that you are not sure that you will enjoy doing or that may be too difficult for you to accomplish. Hereafter, we will refer to your product or service as your 'product'.

2. **Research your market.** Is there really a market for your product, or are you just dreaming? Is there a market in your area, or will you have to move somewhere else? What is the possible size or value of the market in terms of the possible sales or billings per time period, in terms of money. After all, you are going into business to make money. If the market is not real, or it will not provide the amount of money that you need or expect, think of something else. Remember that it is difficult to build a market for something new. Generally, it is not a good idea to start something that will require a lot of

advertising to promote your product. The internet search engines are good tools to use, to research your market. Also it is good to talk to your friends and relatives about your business (as long as you don't give away a good idea.) Talking to others can sometimes help you in important ways. Maybe there is something you did not think of. Or maybe you will get an even better idea in the course of discussion. But don't let anyone discourage you either, especially when they do not have a basis for their comments.

3. **Cost your product.** You need to determine whether or not you can make a profit marketing your product. If you are selling a tangible item, can you sell it at a high enough price to make a profit? Or is the cost of materials and processing so high that making a profit will be difficult? Calculate your profit margin on a sale. Estimate the sales volume. Your profit will be the product of your profit margin and the sales volume divided by 100. For example, if you sell a widget for a dollar, and your material cost is $0.50, your profit margin is 50%. Then if you sell 1000 widgets a day, your profit is 50 times 1000 divided by 100, or $500 each day. If you only sell 100 widgets a day, then your profit is $50 per day. If you are

selling a service, you will have to consider how much your time is worth. For example, if a job you do for someone takes you 10 hours to complete and you can only charge $50 (as the most the market will bear for that kind of work), then you are only making $5 per hour. In the US, you will do better by just getting a job at a McDonalds. The additional factor to consider is whether or not you will have enough jobs or customers for your service in a given time. For example, if my service charge is $10 and I complete it in only ½ hour, I will make $20 per hour for that job. But if I can only sell my service six times a week, I will only make $60 per week. That amount of money might be good as part time work, but hardly enough to provide a living. Finally, make sure you are not paying too much for your materials, or that you spend too much time working inefficiently. If you are doing a service, think out the steps in your work and make sure that you are doing it as efficiently as possible. Do you need better equipment to work more efficiently? Is there a cheaper way to do your work? Can you work faster without over-extending yourself?

4. **Price your product.** How should you price your product? One rule of thumb is to price your product at twice the cost of

the sum of materials and labor. To determine the cost of labor, you need to determine an hourly rate for your time. How much is your time worth to you as described above. If you have an employee or more than one, you need to use the average of the hourly rates, adding in the cost of any benefits you provide such as health insurance, vacation pay, and any other costs associated with that employee. If it is just you doing the work, don't forget to price in your total annual costs to live including all expenses, insurance, food, and anything other expenses you have. If you have another job or source of income, use only that portion of your expenses that you want your new business to cover. One way to calculate the basic product cost is to sum all of the material and expense costs for a full year of sales, and then divide the sum by the number of units or widgets you estimate that you will sell in a years time. Once you have the result, the total cost for each widget you sell, the rule of thumb is to double the cost. The result is then the price that you might sell your product at. A simple example is as follows; Suppose it will cost you $25,000 in materials and expenses to run your business for a year. Also you need another $25,000 to live on during the year. So your total cost and expenses is $50,000. Suppose further that you expect to sell 50,000 widgets in the year (based on your market research.) So then your cost per widget is $1. Then using our doubling rule, you might set the price at $2 each. As time progresses, and you have a better idea of how many items you sell each day or each week on the average, you should recalculate the estimated cost per item or product sold, and revise your price accordingly. Now keep in mind that your price calculation may have to be adjusted, especially if you have stiff competition and someone else is pricing their similar product below the price you calculated. If this is the case you have to decide whether to price your item, less than, equal to, or more than your competition. It is not a good idea to have a price higher than competition unless you have a superior product and people are willing to pay more to buy it.

5. **Legal considerations.** Before you start, make sure you have researched all of the legal requirements for producing and selling your product. If you are the sole business owner, you will probably decide to be a sole proprietor. Or you might want to incorporate. If you decide to incorporate you should only pick either an LLC (Limited Liability Corporation) or an S-Corporation. The reason is that you

want to pass your income from the business directly to your personal bank account to obtain income from your business. I recommend the LLC or S-Corporation to give you protection from law suits. The next thing to decide on is to get all of the licenses you need to operate, local, and state as required. Consult a lawyer if you are not sure of the requirements. Finally, in some businesses, such as any home or business services, you need to be insured and bonded. You can get business insurance from almost any insurance company. Your bond can be obtained from a bonding company that will check your background and verify (or not) that you are eligible to be bonded. You should also have liability insurance as a part of your business protection.

6. **Accounting.** You need to set up your accounting practices. Describing an accounting system in detail is beyond the scope of this book. However, basically you need to record your expenses each day and your revenue each day. You also need to keep a record of any inventory of goods you keep, recording any additions and withdrawals and their value in cash. Also keep a record of cash and try to calculate your total income each month as revenue less expenses. If you have equipment you have invested in, it must

be recorded as an asset and depreciated yearly in accordance with standard accounting practice. A separate record needs to be kept of any sales tax you collect as required by your local and state laws. Of course you also need to keep good records of the sales tax payments you make to the state and/or local governments. If you have employees, you will need a good payroll system. Unless you are a Certified Public Accountant (CPA), you better find one to help you setup your system.

7. **Taxes.** Be aware that you will have to file a tax return to the government, and state as required. When you are operating a business you could be audited by the government tax service so you must have very good and detailed records proving what your income or loss is. Here is another place where you may need professional help to prepare your returns. Again, finding a good CPA may be in your best interest. I use one and the expense is well worth the good tax refunds I usually get back. A lot of times a professional can find you deductions to claim that a business owner might not think about, or even know about. Again, don't forget to remit sales taxes as required.

8. **Social Security.** You should apply to be in the Social Security System. You will have to pay for this benefit, but it is a good back stop when you retire, especially if a person has had financial reverses and needs money to survive. You should also make sure you have good medical insurance for yourself and your immediate family. New federal health requirements may require you to carry health insurance for your employees also. Another reason to only use contract workers to avoid the expense.

9. **Insurance.** If you have a family that depends on you, you should have a term life insurance policy that protects your family in case of your untimely death for whatever reason, at least until you reach retirement age. Another type of insurance to consider is long term care insurance. If you are going to buy it, you will not be able to obtain it if you have developed any significant disease, such as diabetes, hypertension, heart trouble, or any other potentially fatal disease. So, if you decide you need long term care insurance (to protect your estate for your descendents), you should get it around age 50 to 60, before you develop any of the diseases that the insurance company will reject you for.

10. **Safety.** You need to make sure your product is safe for your customers to use or consume. For example, if you have a sandwich truck, you have to be very careful about sanitation and make sure your food is not contaminated in any way. A customer that gets sick on your product will not come back. Also, if you do have a food service, you will most likely be subject to periodic or random Health Department inspections. If you are making a widget of some kind, you must make sure that product cannot cause injury due to some fault in the product. A good example is the toys that had small parts that could choke a child. Or the toys and other items from overseas that were contaminated with toxic materials such as lead or other chemicals. If you are trying to market a processed food product of some kind that would be sold to the general public, you will have to get FDA approval.

11. **Security.** If you are starting a 'brick and mortar' business where you will have a building that houses your product inventory, manufacturing, or some kind of business requiring a building, you will most likely have to apply a security system such as a burglar alarm, surveillance cameras, and so forth. With a 'brick and mortar' business you will most

likely be getting into big money which is probably not your intention if you are reading this book.

12. **Naming your company.** It is important that when you establish a name for your company that you are not copying or duplicating someone else's company name. You could be sued even if your company name is only similar to someone else's. One way to avoid problems is to use your name as part of your company's name. This is what is usually done when a business is a sole proprietorship business. Otherwise, make sure you do a good search on Google or some other search engine to make sure you are not duplicating a name.

Other related books by Roger K. Daneth:

Starting a Business, How to Start a Business, Own Your Own Business. 2011 Kindle eBook.

Stock Investing for Income and Capital Gain. 2011 Kindle eBook.

The Employee's Handbook, How to Survive a New Job. 2011 Kindle eBook.

Career Builder and Handbook. 2011 Kindle eBook.

Find a Job, Find the Job, Keep the Job. 2011
Kindle eBook.

A New You. 2011 Kindle eBook.

Health and Fitness for You and Your Family.
2011 Kindle eBook.

www.ingramcontent.com/pod-product-compliance
Lightning Source LLC
Chambersburg PA
CBHW020858180526
45163CB00007B/2551